Clark & Sharon -
Keep the faith.
Rick

8-5-22

THE PANE OF FAITH

A PILGRIM JOURNEY

RICHARD SIVERS

THERESA BONDGREN

PUBLISHED BY FASTPENCIL PUBLISHING

The Pane of Faith

First Edition

Print edition ISBN: 9781499906714

Copyright © Richard H. Sivers 2020

http://www.fastpencil.com

Printed in the United States of America

TABLE OF CONTENTS

"We do not know that at the center of our being we find
not ourselves but another, that our identity is in another,
that turning inwards and finding ourselves is to fall into
the arms of another."

Ernesto Cardenal (born 1925)

Very special thanks to Terry Bondgren, artist, educator
and friend who executed the cover and all the drawings in
the book.

Chapter One: The Beginning

Dawn broke, but morning seemed to linger far behind it. Only the clock disclosed the reality of time, for all the earth seemed suspended in the darkness of the night which held an unrelenting grasp upon the daylight as it struggled to appear. Everything was caught in an in-between reality, with night attempting to continue its ominous hold on its worldly, dark domain, while morning, by the sheer reality of the constant rotation of the earth, slowly and persistently drove the dark back into its nightly cycle. It was morning, and finally morning began to show itself.

The gray veil, the remnant of the night, began to lift and rays of sunlight filtered into the crisp morning air. The silence was broken by the gentle chirping of birds longing for the day to begin and with the passing moments, flowers raised their blossomed heads to greet the sun. The dew on the blades of grass sparkled like diamonds, and in the far-off field, a deer walked about, nibbling at its breakfast.

Getting out of bed to face the day is always made easier with the glow of morning sunrise and this day was no different. A day of idle "whatevers" lie ahead for me, so there was no need to hurry. I simply waited for the day to beckon me to rise up and engage myself in my duties. On this day, the list of obligations was short, so there was no need to rush about the house checking off accomplished tasks. Instead, I could seek out the leisure joys the day might bring. Any day off from all the tedious responsibilities of work was a welcome treat. Today was to be that day.

The day of the week was irrelevant. Nighttime and daylight know no weekly calendar, so it was a day no different from the countless others that had come and gone; except, today would be different in every way, I just didn't know it yet. I maneuvered my way through all the daily necessities each morning brings and settled into a comfortable chair that looked out onto the deck facing east. It wasn't my favorite chair and I had no intention of staying in it for very long. Just a quick glance across the countryside and then to those few tasks I had set as necessary for the day: some cleaning, a few phone calls, and then the opportunity to choose what leisure pleasure I might enjoy for the remainder of the day.

I perused my yard, and the field and hillside beyond it, was content that all was as it should be, then set to my domestic chores. The morning passed quickly as each job moved from the "to do" column in my head to the completed column. The time had come to relax. A bowl of hot soup to chase away the daytime chill that hadn't seemed to want to be shaken from its hold on even the noontime air, and then to a good book for the afternoon. Reading had always been a great passion, a way to escape. Nothing too serious or educational, just a light novel to take me away from the weariness of a world caught in the grip of constant tensions. Having finished a book a few days before, I picked up the book next on the shelf, settled into my recliner, my favorite chair, and began what was planned to be a relaxing afternoon. Those days of carefree reading so often eluded me that I was determined today to read as much as I could. My eyes poured over line after line of print. An occasional quiet chuckle and even once an outburst of laughter was all the sounds that were heard to invade my private space.

Suddenly a different sound caught my attention. It was the gentle drop, drop, drop of rain on the window panes. I hadn't even noticed the gradual disappearance of the sun as the rain clouds arrived to shroud the blue sky from view. Putting down the book and turning on a couple of lights, I walked to the sliding glass doors to the deck and I caught a glimpse of the sky. It was a light gray hue and I could see through it to where the sun was attempting to open up a vent for its bright rays. Success was on the side of the solar orb, and its golden beams split open the gray blanket, tossing back the feathery clouds to expose the bright blue above. The rain had been just one of those passing showers and I searched the horizon for a rainbow. This day there was none. Perhaps the fleeting raindrops had dispersed too quickly to catch refracted rays and birth a rainbow. I had seen them often, and they always brought a smile to my face. For me they signaled a fresh beginning, but then not every day can offer those kinds of opportunities to in some way start fresh. I shrugged my shoulders in regret for today was not to be one of those days. As I turned from the door to return to my book, out of the corner of one eye I saw something unusual.

Within the few minutes I stood there at the glass door, the gray clouds had totally given way to a canopy of blue, and across the distant hills at the edge of my property, a new cloud appeared. As black as the starless night sky, this cloud, like rolling fog encroaching on a lakeshore, rose above the hillside. It seemed to unfold from within itself, growing ever wider and deeper until all the horizon was consumed by a mournful pitch of colorlessness. Entranced, I watched as the black mantle marched on until it had overcome the light and all the surrounding landscape sank into a shapeless and shadowless oblivion. I stood watching, transfixed to the phenomenon, wondering what was happening. Was I in the center of some violent storm that was about to unleash its fury on the land and on me? My feet were unmoved as the darkness sank deeper and deeper around me and the world outside my sheltered person seemed to disappear. Then a light appeared. Appearing at first with a sudden burst of light, it cast shadows across the lawn and in the room all around me as if the light were coming from every direction. Then the light faded.

Beyond my deck, the mantle that had covered all of life lifted, only slightly enough to see. My feet loosened from their hold to the floor and I took a step back searching the world outside for some sign that what had been was still there. Yes, it was there; the deck, the lawn, but I could see no further. I wavered back and forth and up and down attempting to get a better perspective on the outside world. My eyes squinted, and my head leaned back and forth. There was something there that had not been there before. I looked harder and harder until my eyes were able to focus on the figure of a man. I shook my head, then looked again. There were two images. I closed my eyes, lowering my chin to my chest. I felt disbelief in what I had seen. Dare I open my eyes again? Slowly, apprehensively, I opened my eyes and lifted my head. It had been no trick; the two images were still there.

There in the glass was my reflection-one I had often seen before. When the light was just right, I could see myself in the glass. Like a cloudy mirror, it reflected my image in the midst of all that could also be seen through the glass. So it was this time as well. My faint reflection stared back at me, a look of disbelief on my face, as out on the lawn, a short distance away, I could see myself standing, with outstretched arm beckoning me to come out. I, without fear, instinctively reached for the handle on the door to slide it open, but before my hand could reach the door, I saw my distant image disappear. Confused, I stepped back and the image reappeared. I felt caught in some unexplainable puzzle of conflicting realities. There I was standing in my home, looking both at myself reflected in the glass while seeing myself outside at the same time. I watched with perplexed thoughts at two images of myself.

The vision of myself, at that time was all it seemed to me to be, then motioned with both hands, signaling me to step back away from the door. I could see the quizzical look on my face reflected in the glass, but I obeyed the instruction and stepped back. It was then I heard it for the first time. A voice urged me to close my eyes. I looked around, but there was no one in the room, or, I was quite certain in the house. I was unsure if the voice had come from within my own sense of urgency and confusion, for it sounded so familiar, or if it was real, for it seemed not to be from somewhere else, but around me and within me at the same time. It was a voice I would hear many more times, but in that moment of uncertainty about nearly everything that was happening, I did as I was told.

Before my eyes closed, I saw a light engulfing my distant self. It was neither flame nor from some external source, but it seemed to come from every part of the figure. I thought, the source of a lightning bolt was the gathering of energy from within to then blast forth toward some target. Its brightness so focused it held a purity about it that once unleashed might dispel all darkness and evil. I could sense its building to a crescendo and in the instant I closed my eyes it burst loose. At that moment I felt a wave a calming warmth rush over and through me and when it dissipated, I slowly and cautiously opened my eyes.

I stood there looking once again at my reflection, but the figure that had stood on the lawn was gone. I was not surprised that all that remained was the black void. I searched through the glass to see if I was missing anything, but there was no one there. I sighed a sad sigh and stepped back away from the door further into the room. Suddenly I stopped and looked again at the pane of glass. Instead of seeing only my reflection, I saw two of me, one behind the other. A shudder ran through my body from head to foot like a violent wave hitting a break wall. I turned and stood face-to-face with a lightly veiled image of myself. My legs went numb and I slumped to the floor, faint, but still conscious.

"Let me help you up," he said. "I know this is quite a shock, but don't be afraid." I wasn't. "What you saw outside was indeed yourself, me. Now I am here with you." The voice rang clear, a gentle tone to every word. It was the voice I had heard only a few minutes before. It was me, but not me.

"What's happening?" I asked.

"You will understand soon enough. We are going to go on a journey, a pilgrimage to find your true self."

I wasn't sure what that meant, and I wasn't certain if I needed to find my true self. I thought I already knew who I was, but looking at this image of me, I began to have doubts. "Why?" I was finally able to ask.

"In life we each must uncover the truth about ourselves, our identity and purpose. The time has come for you to make that journey."

"Why now, at my age? Why not when I was younger? And how?"

"That is not for you to know at this moment. It will be made clear with each step you take along the way. Right now, I have a task for you. In order for us to begin this journey, you must find your sacred center, the place where I exist within you."

"I don't understand," I uttered in disbelief.

"You see, within each person is a place where God exists. It is deep within you, far from all the pain and hurts of this world. It is a place of serenity and peace. This place where God is, was infused with your very being, for in many ways it is you, all people; but it is also a part of God, given to you."

"So how do I find this sacred center?"

I sat, as told to do, closed my eyes and listened as I was instructed. First, I had to clear my head of all outside thoughts and distractions. I listened as the voice told me to reach deep within myself to a place of calm, a place of happy memories. Seconds ticked by into minutes and minutes became irrelevant as time passed by as I moved deeper and deeper into myself. I felt a real sense of serenity unlike any I had felt before, hoping that I might stay in that state of peace. But, at long last the voice grew quiet. I had arrived. There was a return of the warmth I had felt before, a sense of fulfillment. I inhaled a deep breath, slowly let it out and opened my eyes. I was alone once again. I stood, looked out the glass door at the blackness for a moment, then the voice, inside of me, said simply, "The time has come to begin. We are one. Now step to the glass." I hesitated. Curiously looked at the time on my watch: 1:38 pm. "Now step through the pane of glass." I hesitated to take the step, but then without equivocation or fear, together, as one, we stepped through the pane of glass.

Chapter Two: Into the Glass

I've never been certain if I stepped through the glass or into it. It is a mystery never to be solved. None-the-less, my action was to do as I had been told, and step through the glass. Perhaps that meant through only the outer surface rather than completely through the entire pane of glass. Once again, attempting to rationally unravel all the mysteries I encountered has become an exercise in futility. I don't have the answers, they were never revealed to me, and ultimately, they were answers I never needed. I was there to "find myself" and that, in itself, would prove to be a monumental undertaking.

Stepping into or through the glass, while a painless experience, left me suspended between where I had been and where I finally would go. It was the same dark world I had seen earlier descend upon my home. Before I had seen it as a void, with an ominous encroachment on my world, now I stood within it. There was no sense of foreboding, no fear, not even a hint of apprehension; just wonder. There I stood, with nothing to support my feet or hold me in place. I could move and even walk around, always without resistance to my movements. It seemed like I had descended into a giant cask of black gelatin that supported my every move but did not impede me in any way. I felt nothing touching me and outside my own movements, no sense of motion. To say that it was black may not be totally true, for it possessed no color and no light appeared to penetrate it. If I was being ushered from one place to another, I had no sensation of it happening.

After some time, although I have no way of knowing how long it was, an instant of creeping anxiety began to bubble up within me. To counter it, I thought of my sacred center and the serenity I had felt back in my living room. For it wasn't a describable place, no beach or comfortable chair. Rather, just a sense of overall calm, not unlike the feeling of lying in bed in the silence of the night with no thoughts to occupy the mind. I covered my eyes with my hands as if to block out any light, even though there was none. The darkness was now of my making, and I felt my heart rate slow as I was reunited with myself at my sacred center. Together we dispelled the temptation to move into a state of fear. Time passed, once more at a pace I could not decipher, and when I removed my hands from my eyes, I could see a glow of light.

First near my feet, like a platform, and then around me, pushing back the darkness. It was then I realized what I had been experiencing may have been no more than a few seconds, elongated in my mind by both the awe and amazement of the situation. Gradually the darkness retreated revealing a cocoon of light. Swirling faster than I could calculate, the light opened up the tomb of blackness that had encompassed me to unveil an arena of pure light. I stood at its center, a space no larger than fifteen feet in diameter, flooded by the light of the walls, floor and ceiling that contained me. I spun around and around, but it was the same no matter where I looked. I stopped to try to take it all in when a shudder ran through me and I sensed my inner self had stepped out from my body. I turned and he was there. I would come to know that sensation, that shudder that rippled through me very well; yet, I always found it difficult to look at myself, not as a reflection, but as a separate reality.

"What now?" I asked. "Where are we?" I restated the questions, "Where am I?"

"You are at the center of where all creation exists. You are in the presence of God." He paused. "It's difficult to explain."

"Try," I pleaded, not understanding how my other self could hold such knowledge without my knowing.

"Sit down," he said, and we sat facing each other as the light continued to circle around us. "Let me put it this way," he began. "God is a force, a power; a living presence everywhere. While within God there is no heart or brain, no physical being as you would understand it, there is a reality on another dimension. We are now in the midst of that presence. Where normally all of life is on the periphery, held in place by the power of the omnipotent God, you have been brought to the center of that power. The light you see around us is where the inner being of God both starts and stops. Beyond the light are many worlds, in different dimensions, on different planes. Some worlds, like your earth, move in measured time, while others exist in a different time frame all kept in balance by God's will. Sometimes God chooses to bring individuals from their world and their reality into another, to experience a higher level of understanding. God chose you to enter into that realm of discovery in the midst of God's omniscience. Does that help?"

"Some, I guess. But where am I, really? Am I in the glass, or did I pass through it?"

"When you stepped through the glass you passed through one side into a place that is neither here nor there, neither outside the glass nor inside it." He paused again noting the confused look on my face. "I suppose that didn't help at all. You see the pane of glass is merely a tool to allow worlds to change; to open up a space between what is on one side and the other. That is why you can see both your reflection in the glass and what lies on the other side at the same time. You have been brought to a place that is between both what you can see and what you are. Here you are not of your world, but you are the world, because now you are one with God."

"Why?" I couldn't seem to muster much more to ask than that.

"Because God has a task for you. You are going on a pilgrimage, and along the way your fears and doubts will surface within you in order to bring to light your strengths through faith in yourself and in God."

"Does this happen to many others?"

"More than you could ever know. Now to explain what is going to happen. You will be given a series of challenges, pathways to follow to test both your physical existence and your spiritual actuality. You will participate in one, the physical, and I the other. When you have completed each task, we will be reunited for a time of meditation and contemplation. When all the tasks have been completed, we will go back to your home where we will be joined as one for the rest of your earthly life."

"I'm afraid." It was my first acknowledgement of any fear about the experience. "I'm not very clever, no real skills and physically, well, I'm no athlete."

"That doesn't matter. For every task you will be able to assemble all the necessary tools to reach the end. God will not put before you anything you cannot complete. This is all for you to succeed; there can be no failure. Stepping into the pane of glass has set you on a journey between two worlds, the physical and the spiritual. Your feet will be firmly grounded in the familiarity of the world into which you were born, while I will transcend that world to journey on a plane that is beyond your known world. Together we will see deeper into who you are than you ever could see on your own. It will be as if you were one person experiencing two very different realities at the same time. Are you ready to begin?"

There was a slight hesitation in my answer. I had never been one to seek out new experiences in life, preferring to live within my comfort zone. Now I had been given an opportunity to explore who I was, an opportunity I would never have again. "I suppose so. What's going to happen next?"

"The light will slowly part revealing an opening through which you will pass. As you walk through that opening the light will close behind you and you will find yourself in a place where you will have to find the pathway and seek what is there for you to discover."

"What does that mean?"

"I can't say what you will discover. I will remain here, but even though we are separated from each other I will experience what you experience but from a spiritual perspective, helping you as I can. Remember, no matter what, you are not alone. I am with you. I believe the time has come. Watch for the opening. When you have discovered all that there is to find, you will feel the need to rest and will be returned here with me."

I sat looking for that opening to appear, turning my head from side to side until at last the curtain of light began to slowly open, wider and wider at the bottom then the top. It was like a great theater curtain opening to reveal a stage set for some never before seen production, and I was to be an actor in the play. I could see nothing beyond the opening until I stepped outside the cocoon of light and found myself standing on a grassy hillside. Turning around, I saw the cocoon of light from which I had just stepped, disintegrate like specks of dust swirling on the breeze in the rays of sunlight.

Chapter Three: Pathway Through the Valley

There I stood looking out on a wide expanse of valley. Hills rose steeply to my right and left, cascading back into a valley lush with a carpet of green. There were no trees, just acres and acres of undulating grass, bowing to the insistence of a gentle breeze blowing from behind me down through the length of the valley. From where I stood, I saw no end before or behind me. The knoll on which I stood seemed positioned in the middle of an eternal view. The sky above was bright with blue, although I could see no sun to light it, and no matter where I looked, no shadows. At my feet, only grass, but no sign of any direction defined by a gray silhouette cast by light. Here there was no east, south, west or north to give me location; only me standing in the midst of nowhere.

"What do I do now?" I whispered aloud, fully expecting my other self to answer. Silence! He had said he would be with me throughout each experience, but at that moment I felt a detachment. Was this all some dream, a ruse to shatter my understandings and cause a breakdown for some cruel, unknown reason? It was then I recognized that I would have to press on, alone if necessary, to find a conclusion to this first challenge, and that is how I saw it. I was now in competition with myself, and I had to find that key that would unlock the answer to why I had been sent to this place.

I decided that just standing still was not an appropriate option and I moved down the knoll into the valley. Perhaps there I would find the answers to my journey. I hesitated to call it a quest, but instead to think in terms of an ongoing journey or pilgrimage as he had told me when I had begun. So, I began my journey into the valley. The sweeping arch of the hills rose at my sides as I walked further and further into the valley ahead of me. The grass lay down beneath the pressure of each step I took and the child in me urged me to stop and remove my shoes and socks and continue on barefoot. I found there were no stones, no sharp edges to injure me in any way, only the soft coolness of the blades of the green coverlet on the ground.

As I reached the nadir of the valley, I found a meandering stream. Clear, unpolluted water babbled across the streambed stones, flowing relentlessly from an unknown source in the hills emptying into some distant, unseen depository. It was then, looking down at the water, that the water, the grass, even the air, were all pristine with no life within them. There were no birds singing or winging their way through the air; no insects buzzing; no minnows or other life in the stream. What appeared on the surface to be a green paradise was in fact a valley of nothingness. I bent down and pulled gently at a few blades of grass which easily came free within my fingers' grip and then disappeared. My hand splashed the water. I cupped my hands to draw some water from the stream and as I lifted my hands the water disappeared from view.

I sat down, frustrated by the mixture of signs: lush valley, no shadows, no other life. My head sank down into my open hands. I felt the confusion of the moment overwhelm me with despair. My shoulders slumped toward the ground as I felt myself slip further away from my journey and into an isolated world with no apparent options. I was already giving up. The disengagement from finding a solution had come so soon.

Challenges had never been easy for me. Small ones could be met with some degree of fortitude, but those life-altering possibilities were never faced head on but danced around until some easier option revealed itself. Now I faced a situation I had to master, and if this was the first of many that I had to face and could not master it, how was I to overcome the others? Amid the despair and disappointment. I felt a wave of anger; not with myself, but the situation. I stood up, shouting as if there was someone besides myself to listen to my angry list of grievances.

Anger was not an emotion I had utilized in my life, preferring a more stable emotional track, using pacifism to achieve good ends. But now I was angry with the world around me and the God who had sent me there.

"What is this all about?" I shouted. "What am I to do? Walk around endlessly scouring the landscape for a sign I might not recognize even if I found it? Oh, God, help me." With those words I fell to the ground. Now I was angry not only with God, but myself. I was in a situation I was totally unprepared to face. Alone, no visible options, no rational solutions, I had failed; or so I thought.

Yet, I resolved not to fail, but to succeed. If standing still had solved nothing, I would run, traversing the valley until I found the answer. So I put on my socks and shoes and ran. Then I jogged, I walked and then ran some more. My anger fueled my determination. I followed the path of the stream that zig-zagged through the valley, ran up and down the hillsides all until I was breathless. Nothing! No sign, no hint of an answer, but I would not be beaten. I would not succumb to some invisible negative force either outside of me or within me.

Resting, bent over with my hands resting on my knees, I began to question if there was an answer. My mind returned to thoughts of trickery and games that singled me out as a pawn and once again I was overwhelmed by feelings of unknowing and disappointment. My adversary, despair, was winning the battle over me and I slumped to the ground. I rolled over onto my back, realizing the celestial dome above me was darkening. The world was closing in on me. Tears left my eyes and rolled down my cheeks. It was over, I had failed after all. The darkness descended on the valley and I slipped away in sleep.

When I awoke, I found myself back in the cocoon of light with my other self looking at me. His face was ashen, and he looked exhausted.

"Do I look as bad as you?" I asked.

"You do. We have both been through a great deal."

His words confused me. "Where were you?" I asked as I sat up. "You said you would always be with me, but you weren't there."

"I was with you, but on a spiritual level only. Our two realities could not meet."

He sounded like someone trying to escape capture in some wild scheme. "Why didn't you tell me that? I waited. I looked for you. I ran around like a madman, but I found nothing. Nothing! I failed."

"You didn't fail," he reassured me.

"But I found nothing," I repeated with a descending tone of disappointment.

"You found a part of yourself."

"What?" I asked with bewilderment.

"You found a part of yourself. That's what this is all about. It isn't about finding things, tangible things, but what's inside of you, yourself."

"What about you? What did you find?

"I found a piece of you."

"Explain."

"I saw you enter a lush, green valley and discover that you were the only living thing there. I felt your pain, your anger, your despair."

"What about you, where were you?

He paused and a sullen look came over him. "My valley was a barren one, but not like yours. I felt the pain of stones bruising my feet and the harassment of insects. With your inner pain I ached beyond anything I could ever imagine. With your anger I grew weaker, but with your despair I found hope."

"That doesn't make sense."

"But it does. Despair can be unforgivingly debilitating. The lack of hope leads us to a darkness. Recovery opens the portal to the light of hope. Faith guides the feet and grace unlocks the door."

"But I had no hope. All I felt was despair. There was no success."

"In sinking as low as you did you opened a door for hope. You had faced an obstacle, a task in ways you never had before in your life. Your tears were the sign that you were reaching out. No words were needed. In your aloneness, in facing the challenge you didn't run away from it, but toward it. Sometimes there is no visible adversary, only our own inner fears and doubts. You have now begun to better understand yourself. The pain I suffered was what was released from within you, transferred to me. The opening allowed your despair to be replaced by hope. Do you feel it?"

I wasn't certain what hope was supposed to feel like, but I admitted I felt less hesitant now about myself.

"You, we have taken the first step together. Now we need to rest to be replenished for the next part of our journey. Close your eyes and go back to your sacred center that together, as one, we might be strengthened for what lies ahead."

I closed my eyes, rest was welcomed. I could feel him enter me as I moved to that sacred place within where we were safe together.

Chapter Four: Pathway Through the Forest

I awoke with a start, feeling that quizzical shudder as he left me. Instinctively I looked at my watch to see what time it was, but the watch had stopped, I supposed at the time I stepped through the glass.

"Time is irrelevant here," he said. "Where we are, there is no time, at least not as you know it. What seems like a forever, may be only an instant, and vice-versa." My body ached and I felt exhausted by the experience, even though I knew I had slept for some time. I relaxed and fell asleep once more, sleeping in a cocoon of contentment. Surrounded by a silence of comfort, I drifted away for the rejuvenation necessary to continue.

When I awoke once more, there I lay, looking at myself seated beside me in a quiet calm, staring down at me. I stretched out of my fetal position and sat up.

"Now what?" I asked. My question seemed a repeat of so many others I had either thought or asked before, but somehow knew the answer would not be conclusively clear.

"Are you ready for what comes next?" He smiled. I sensed his anticipation and realized I was already starting to stand before I answered.

"For whatever comes my way."

"Good, because what happens next will be more difficult than what you have already experienced." That filled me with dread, remembering what I had endured.

"Will each stage be more difficult than the last?"

"Perhaps, perhaps not. It all depends on you." He paused one of those "I don't think I should say anything more" moments of silence. I positioned myself, as I had before, and waited for the veil of light to open. Once again, like some great thick impenetrable drapery, the light parted. I took a deep breath, closed my eyes and stepped through into the unknown. As I did, I heard him say, "Together."

There was no eager anticipation in opening my eyes this time; but hearing the chirping of birds and the rustle of leaves, caused me to rethink my need for hesitation and I opened my eyes. I twirled around in amazement. Unlike the lifeless, artificial look and feel of the valley, now I found myself in the midst of a dense forest teeming with life. I reached out to touch all that I could to reassure myself it was real: leaves, tree trunk, grass, even overturning a flat stone at my feet only to see an earthworm descend out of sight. Birds sang their songs, butterflies fluttered by, insects made themselves known all around me.

They seemed somehow familiar, yet, strange to the senses. Standing still was impossible as I sought to explore the secrets of this woodland mystery. Choosing a direction to travel didn't seem to matter, so I scanned the ground to see if any path appeared. No footprints, paws or hooves revealed themselves; the grass unbent by the weight of any passersby. I moved in the direction between two large maple trees, smiling as I explored. Sunlight filtered down through the umbrella of leaves, igniting the colors of blossoms below, butterflies and all things that moved. There was a job here, no intrusion of anything ominous.

As I moved along, I touched the trunks of trees, bent down to smell flowers, reaching out to experience everything around me. My senses longed for fulfillment and I tried to absorb all I could as I moved slowly along. Coming upon an unusually beautiful rose bush in full bloom, I paused, reached down and picked one of the blossoms to take in its fragrance. Surprisingly, the blossom withered and disintegrated in my hand. Yet, the stem where it had been attached, simultaneously brought forth an identical blossom. My forehead furrowed with perplexity.

"What are you thinking?" I looked up and there I stood, hands at my hips staring at me.

"What just happened?" I asked.

"I have no idea. All I wanted to do was smell the flower. Then it was gone."

"I thought we couldn't be together? That you were in some other distant place?"

"I am. What you see is merely an image that you think you need to see; but you truly have no need to see me now." With that, the image began to fade.

"But the flower? What about the flower?" He was gone, and I was once more alone.

"Now what am I supposed to do?" I asked out loud, knowing I was the only one who could hear and answer. Perhaps it was just that one blossom that could be restored, Perhaps, in my own random choice, I had picked the one rose that was particularly designed to regenerate. It didn't really make sense to me, but I tested the theory by picking a flower from a different bush. Once again, the flower vanished in my hand as a new blossom appeared on the stem. I picked a flower off the forest garden floor, with the same result. It was then I looked back to find there were no signs of where I had stepped along my pathway, no broken twigs, no bent blades of grass. All that I had disturbed had been restored. That gave me comfort; that in this place I could do no harm.

While I knew in my heart it was not a reflection of real life, it instilled in me an inner joy. This place was one of continual triumph over destruction. I longed that this were the real world, one where all things good and beautiful were perpetuated; a form of harmony that had no end. I assured myself I could use that hope when I returned home. But for now, I had to move on.

I walked on further into the forest, passing through both thick underbrush and open glens, always being careful not to break any branches or damage plants. Even though I knew if I did cause any destruction, it would be "repaired." And, it was each time. I convinced myself I shouldn't be the cause of any destructive behavior. As I observed, each bent twig straightened, and each flattened blade of grass returned to standing upright. I mused that the forest, even with all its strangeness, was reminiscent of woodlots from my childhood adventures. I dismissed the thought, thinking that all forests and woodlots probably had a certain familiarity about them, and this truly was a place I had never seen before.

Minutes of walking turned into hours–at least so it seemed. Occasionally, I stopped to look up through the canopy of leaves and branches, catching glimpses of the azure sky above. The sound of birds calling to one another along with the flutter of wings often broke the silence. I felt like whistling or singing, but caught myself before I did, realizing the sounds I made were an intrusion on the beauty and serenity of the forest. I let the sounds of nature dominate.

Without even noticing, I suddenly found myself facing a towering wall of vines. The heavily wooded vines grew out of the ground tangling with one another in a symphony of intertwined tendrils clamoring for the warmth of the sunlight above the treetops. Yet, the vines were also like stones that were fitted together to form an impenetrable wall of vine with tentacles securely wrapped around each other and the tree limbs. The spiral feelers reached out to one another, weaving a curtain of green from forest floor to its ceiling.

There was no hesitation for me, so I began the ascent. I could feel some of the vines groaning under the stress of my weight, yet none gave way. The climb to the top was filled with anticipation, an inner exhilaration that made its way to hands and feet grappling for the next hand or foothold. Up and up I climbed until I reached the summit where the forest canopy spread out in all directions as far as I could see. The blue sky, the warm sun and the green carpet that emanated from where I stood were a marvel of nature. Testing the strength of the vines and finding them sturdy, I turned around and lay back on the forest penthouse bed of green. There I lie, musing about this idyllic world of harmony, finally falling asleep basking in the brightness and warmth of daylight.

When I awoke, I was no longer atop my verdant perch, but back inside the cocoon of light staring at myself.

"Must you always be looking at me that way?" I asked as I rose to a sitting position.

"What way?"

"That way. The way you're sitting there. It's like you are staring right through me."

"Is that the way you see me? Does that frighten you?" he asked.

"No, it's just annoying." I stood up and began to circle around him.

"What did you discover?" he asked.

"You should know, you were there."

"Only in your imagination. You thought you needed me, but you didn't. I was in the other place, comfortably assessing all that beauty had to offer. What did you discover about yourself?"

I squatted down beside him. "There is great joy in life; everywhere and in everything. I heard it in the songs the birds sang and in the color of the flowers. Yet, it was all so fragile. I needed to be careful not to destroy anything. But if I did, it came back. I'm not sure what that means. Can you answer that? What did you find?"

"I found the same, but what was damaged was not restored. Still, the joy you felt carried me through the maze and entanglements where I found myself."

"Perhaps the lesson is a little of both. Joy can carry us through life. Even though we don't always see it, nor feel it, it's all around us and we need to preserve it."

With that we both laid down and when I had closed my eyes and my thoughts had found rest, I felt him return to me and together we slept.

Chapter Five: Pathway
Through the Plain

Again, I awoke to the shudder of departure as he left me. My sleep had been more restful than the one before, the previous journey less traumatic than my first.

"I have a couple of questions," I said.

"Ask away, but you know I may not be able to answer them."

"Can't, or won't?"

"Just ask." His reply was spoken very precisely.

"How come I'm not hungry?"

"Remember that time is of no consequence here, so hunger being a bodily function that is relative to time, also has no consequence." His answer made sense to me.

"When you go where you go, what is it like?" I had wanted to ask that from the beginning but was afraid he would not answer.

"It's very hard to explain." He hesitated, stood and paced quietly around our little cocoon. "It is a little like, how do I describe it so you'll understand? A little like being in a lightless elevator. I feel movement, I hear sounds, but I can't ever go anywhere outside that black space. What you feel, I feel. What you hear, I hear. What you see, I see. Although it is less an image and more of a sense of something. That's all I can say." His face grew pale as he walked away from me and then sat with his back to me.

"Are you all right?" I asked, as I moved next to him.

"I'm fine. But I've said too much."

As his words faded away the light beside me began to part and I understood my time to leave was at hand. I stood and looked at him searchingly then stepped through the opening in the light and out of the rest of the cocoon.

When my eyes adjusted to the light of the new surroundings, I found myself on a wide, smooth pathway atop a meandering ridge. With rocks protruding on either side of the pathway, it seemed almost as if I were standing on the backbone of a scaly ancient reptile that had lain down to rest. A strange shifting wind blew from my left and then from my right. I felt the wind against my cheek.

Stretching out to the left of me for as far as I could see was a vast plain of waving grain. Bright golden stalks swayed back and forth in undulating swells and ebbs. It was almost like watching the sun-drenched, golden-capped waves of an ocean moving inward and outward to the horizon. On the opposite side of the ridge, snows swirled across a frozen plain of white starkness. Barren rocks protruded from the icy landscape causing the snows to shift and oscillate above and around the outcroppings. The two areas flanking the ridge were direct opposites of each other. The one side rich and bountiful and the other a bleak desert of snow and ice. My head moved back and forth from side to side, my eyes scanning each plain for an anomaly or sign to their meaning. It was while looking so intently to both my left and my right, that the breeze that was brushing gently across my cheeks had no warmth nor coolness. That puzzled me, for I supposed that any air moving across a warm plain or a frozen tundra would produce in its breezes a temperature swept up from the surface.

I walked forward along the path, my eyes continuing to search for anything within the two plains that would give me a hint to what to do or where I should go. Nothing appeared. Pausing to sit on a large rock that was part of the ridgeline, I debated what to do next. I could continue on the path, in either direction for an endless length of time, proving nothing; I could venture into the plain of waving grain or onto the snowy plain; or, I could decide to do nothing at all. Calculating the consequences of each action, I chose to do nothing.

In that instant I was suddenly swept away from my position on the ridge back into the cocoon of light. The swiftness of the action startled me so much I wasn't certain what had really happened. I felt like I had been wrestled with and then slammed to the floor. I could see my inner self struggling to get up off the floor.

"What just happened?" I asked.

"You tell me," came his response. The blank look on his face must have mirrored my own.

"One second I'm sitting on a boulder resting, and the next I'm back here with you."

"What were you feeling back where you were?" he asked as he settled into a sitting position. I assumed the same position facing him. "I didn't feel anything," I said.

"And I felt torment." He paused. "You didn't feel anything?"

"I felt a breeze, but it didn't feel hot or cold. I suppose now that I think about it, it should have felt like something."

"What about inside? What were you thinking?"

"Isn't that your domain? Aren't you supposed to know all that?"

"Am I?" was his quick retort.

His response caught me off guard. I hesitated, then answered him. "I was thinking I should do nothing."

"Nothing," he said incredulously. "Nothing?"

"I assumed that whether I went forward or backward on the ridge I would be going nowhere. If I went onto the plain where the grain was growing, I would probably lose my way; and, if I ventured onto the frozen plain, I would undoubtedly freeze to death. So, I decided to do nothing. Is that so bad?"

"Your nothingness sent me into torment. Do you have any idea what nothing is?"

"No. But, sometimes doing nothing is the only choice."

He stood and looked down at me with a fierceness in his gaze I had not seen before. "Doing nothing is the conscious choice to avoid making a decision."

"What? That's double-talk."

"Is it?

"Yes, you do something, or you do nothing."

"And what does that prove? What do you gain?"

"Time. You gain time to consider your options. Doing nothing is a choice, a decision."

"Is it?"

"Stop asking that." I stood so we were face-to-face.

"When has doing nothing ever achieved anything that a firm decision to act has not?"

I had no answer. He put his hands on my shoulders and gently pushed me back into a sitting position. He sat looking into my eyes with a fierce look once more.

"Listen to me. Nothing is just that, nothing. I suppose some people would argue the necessity of waiting before acting, but that is not doing nothing." He paused again. "Nothing is a void it is torment without purpose. The consequences of doing nothing is an eternal damnation. You put me in a dark place, and you were headed toward a dark place yourself. That's why it ended when it did."

"Did you know it was going to happen that way?"

I had no sooner completed the question when the wall of the cocoon opened, but unlike before when I had walked through the opening, this time I was pulled out of the cocoon by an unseen force dragging me across the floor out into the space beyond the light.

CHAPTER SIX: PATHWAY THROUGH THE CANYON

I found myself lying face down on the hard-packed barren earth. Spitting out dust from my mouth, I shouted, "What was that all about?" I lifted myself up off the ground. "Now what?" As soon as I said it, I knew it was a foolish question; one whose answer I would have to discern for myself. The thought, "nothing is not an option"

kept running through my head, echoing like the words of a parent chastising a child. "I've got it," I said out loud in an attempt to rid myself of the reoccurring thought, so I could move on with the immediate situation.

Shaking off the dust from the ground as I stood, I looked around and saw myself standing on the floor of a great canyon. While in my last challenge all was flat with vast open spaces to the sky, here I faced towering walls of earth on either side of me. The walls, impregnable rock and earth like nature's skyscrapers, bordered a hollow hallway between their soaring ramparts. There I stood, looking up at the narrow band of blue sky above me; sunlight filtering down not from directly above me, but from one side. To my left, the walls of the canyon gleamed in sunlight, while the walls to my right were veiled in shadows. The contrast between the two walls of the canyon was immediately obvious to me. I walked over to the sunlit wall to examine its composition. From the ground to as high as I could clearly see, layer was stacked upon layer, the stratified layers of earth and stone delineated by color and texture. How marvelous it was to see the earth laid bare, its eons of growth and change exposed to view.

I know enough about archaeology and geology to be able to identify the meaning behind the thicknesses of layers and how the composition of the layers was indicative of environmental conditions that created them. I could see layers of small stones, sand and silt. Some layers were thin while others were thick. Some were more compact than others; some crumbled to the ground below at my touch.

I turned and looked at the opposite canyon wall. From where I stood, the difference between the layers of earth and stone were almost imperceptible. The darkened wall hid its secrets and I wondered if what I saw on the one side would be revealed on the other. A few steps across the canyon floor revealed the answer. The two sides of the canyon were nearly identical with only a few variations in the different strata. My conclusion was that whatever had formed the canyon, wearing away what had joined the two walls, had cut down through the earth exposing the now present walls. One could easily fill in the gap and match up the walls in a continuous layer-upon-layer. I assumed the canyon had been formed, not by some cataclysmic event, but rather by the gradual ravages of time.

There I stood at the bottom of the canyon between the walls, with a narrow canyon stretched out in either direction. At my feet, no visible sign of the flowing water that must have once meandered on land, gradually, almost imperceptibly, day-by-day, carried away the soft earth, leaving behind the canyon. I faced the dilemma of what to do, remembering the admonition that doing nothing was not a choice. I dug my shoe into the hard ground, leaving a visible mark that would serve as my starting point. I began walking.

That which had formed the canyon had created a serpentine, rambling route through the countryside. I couldn't see what lie on the ground above the towering walls, no sign of grass or tree branches leaning over into the canyon as if to spy on what was happening below that would give me a clue to what was in the world beyond where I stood. As I walked through the twisting maze, I realized that no matter what direction the canyon took, the one wall was always sunlit and the other always in shadow. Nothing seemed to change; time truly was standing still. I kept watch of the canyon walls, the undulating layers, their up and down trails like gently rolling hills. Occasionally a stone protruded and while I was tempted to pull them out, I resisted, remembering my experiences in the valley and the forest.

Having walked a considerable distance, what I thought was long enough to see if there were any markers or changes in the canyon, seeing none, I turned around, retracing my steps. When I arrived where I had etched a mark in the ground, I continued on to see if there was anything to discover in the opposite direction. Everything was the same. There were no distinguishing characteristics to be seen and after walking for what I thought was about the same distance that I had covered in the opposite direction, I turned around and walked back to my point of origin.

"If I had been put here, on this spot," I said aloud, "then there must be a reason. If there is nothing different to discover in either direction up or down the canyon, the answer must be up or down." I knelt down and dug with my hands in the parched dirt. With no tools, digging was nearly impossible. I gave up. "Well then," I thought, "I guess I will have to climb up." Scaling the canyon wall would not be easy, but I decided I had to make the effort. Examining each wall again, I chose the wall bathed in light where I would be better able to see; where I would best be able to find my hand and foot holds in the wall.

Some of the layers were soft, easy enough to hollow out for my hand or foot. I began, very slowly. This was not a race, I reminded myself, not a sprint, but a slow climb of discovery. Hand above my head, dislodging soft dirt then pulling myself up while I maneuvered my foot into a separate layer. One hand, a foot, the other hand and other foot, slowly I was scaling the wall. Ten feet, fifteen feet, twenty feet; each milestone giving me a sense of accomplishment. This was something I had never done before, nor had I even entertained the notion of rock-climbing; but I was doing it. I could finally see across the open canyon ledge to what lie beyond, and then I felt my feet and hands come loose from the canyon wall and I began to fall.

As I fell, my thoughts turned to what might have been had I not tried to scale that sheer, vertical wall. Then my mind drifted off as if in sleep. When I awoke, I sat up with a sudden lurch from the position of my back to the floor. I was back in the cocoon. I was startled to find my other self, lying motionless beside me. "What have I done?" I said. But touching him, his stillness turned to gentle motion and he opened his eyes.

"Are you all right?" I asked in a hushed tone. I helped him sit up.

"Yes," he answered.

"Did I do something wrong? Maybe I should have just stayed at the bottom of the canyon, but your words...."

"My words?"

"Nothing is not an option."

"Oh," he said. "That's why."

"What do you mean?" I asked, moving closer to him.

"You made a choice to act, that's good."

"But it almost got us...." I stopped before I could finish.

"Killed?" He finished my sentence.

"Yes."

"That wouldn't have happened. No one dies here. The objective is for everyone to live."

"But you weren't breathing. I thought I might have killed you."

He smiled, one of those gentle, knowing smiles filled with understanding. "I wasn't dead. I was...." He hesitated. "I was partially in you. You were protecting me." There was another long pause. "You did all the right things."

"But I never made it to the top. I never found out what was up there."

"You may not understand this now, but you were not ever going to reach the top. You are not meant to know everything. No one can understand all there is to know. There will always be some mysteries left in life. But whether you realized it or not, when you started to fall, you sheltered yourself with me in your sacred center. I survived because of you, and you survived because of me."

It was then I realized how tired I was. We both simultaneously lay back and fell asleep, joined once more as one.

CHAPTER SEVEN: PATHWAY THROUGH THE DESERT

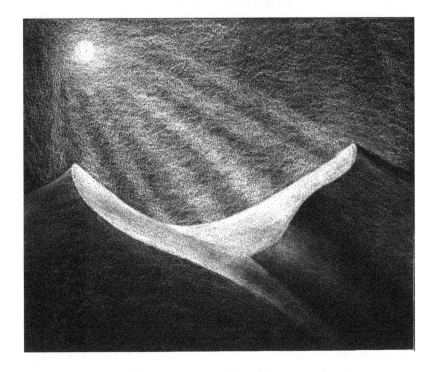

Sleep seemed to endure far beyond its necessity, but when it ended, I felt fully rested.

"I wondered how long you would sleep," he said with a smile. He had left me while I had slept, my sleep so deep I had not felt his withdrawal. Now he stood over me, examining me with an intense gaze. "You must have been deep in sleep when I left. You never stirred. Were you dreaming?"

"I was." I paused and stood. "I'm not sure. Maybe. It's very unclear right now. Sometimes I think I'm dreaming, but I'm not. It's like seeing things, but not being a part of it. That's not very clear is it?"

"I understand. Often what may seem as dreams are in reality visions."

"Visions?" I asked.

"Visions are what God wants you to see, not what you might surface from your subconscious, like a dream."

I put my hand up to stop him. "So, is that all a dream or a vision? Am I back in my house right now experiencing all this in my head?"

"I assure you this is all very real. You are not resting comfortably in your easy chair, but here with me."

"Will I remember all of this? Or, when I go back, will I forget it as if it never happened?" He sensed the anxiety in my voice. I pressed him further. "If I don't remember this, what good has it been?"

"I had hoped we could save this conversation for later, but I suppose now is as good a time as ever. Sit down. I'll explain."

His eyes had changed from that searching gaze to one of personal introspection. I sensed the gravity of the moment and quietly sat waiting for him to speak. Instead of speaking right away, he paced back and forth uncertain of where to begin. At last he sat down facing me.

"Do you remember when you began this journey, I told you, you were in the presence of God?" I nodded affirmatively. "Each time you leave the cocoon you venture deeper into God's reality, into an aspect of your being that requires...." he paused, "some work." I gave him a scowling glance which he immediately understood. "We all need to improve ourselves. Every time you leave the cocoon, a learning experience is set in motion. What you learn, what I learn, will always be with you, with us. You will not remember the details, but instead the lesson; but it will be very real. When you go back home, I will be with you. I will no longer be able to separate myself from you but will be hidden deep within you."

"In my sacred center," I said with a sense of pride that I had remembered.

"Yes. We will forever be one." He paused once more. "But for now, we have to go our separate ways. Look." He pointed to behind me where the walls of the cocoon had begun to open.

"Until we meet again. No, until we see each other again," I said.

I stood and as I walked toward the beckoning open space, I looked back at him and saw a sadness in his face, but there wasn't time to make inquiry about it. I stepped forward, feeling a great rush of air, then the opening closed behind me.

There I stood in the hollow between two sand dunes. A scorching sun beat down on me from above and the reflected light off the sand rose up in waves of undulating hot air. As always, it was time for choosing. To either side of me the dunes stretched out in golden brown mounds. Ahead of me and behind me, the dunes rose to an imposing height; not steeply, but with a gentle incline to a point far above my head. On all sides, I could see waves of heat rippling through the air, rising up and disappearing as the heat diffused in the open spaces above my head.

I learned from my previous experience that now I had to make a choice and commit to it. I decided to climb the dune ahead of me, with the hope that this time, in this adventure, I would reach the top and discover what might lie beyond my current vantage point. So, I set out. The heat was intense, and with each step up the dune I could feel the beads of sweat gathering together all over my body, converging as cascading streams. The ascent up the dune was far longer and more difficult than I had imagined. The grains of sand belched out from beneath my shoes with every step I took. The end result was constant slipping. At first, I reached down to help myself by thrusting my hands into the sands to pull myself forward, but the heat of the sand burned my hands. After that, every time I reached down with my hands, I paused, pulled my hands back, repositioning my body and pressing on with my feet alone.

I felt my strength waning as the heat and exertion began to take their toll. The dune proved to be only the first of two I would have to climb. The second, like the second leg of a marathon race, challenged me even more. Still, I continued on; my skin and clothes drenched with sweat, my legs aching from the stress, my face burned from exposure to the unrelenting sun, and my body longing for water to quench the thirst and dissuade the onslaught of dehydration. The thought of water consumed my thinking as much as the demands I had put upon myself to reach the summit of the dunes.

In an instant my view of the world was obscured by a sudden sandstorm. The wind came from every direction, whipping up the sand into a frenzied whirl of brown clouds. The sand biting my skin as it pummeled my face and clothes. I sank to the ground, covered my head with my arms and waited until the wind subsided and the sand drifted back down to earth. In the darkness of the storm I wondered if it was worth the effort, if I had made a wrong choice, if I had been so determined to climb the dune when it might have been better to stay at the bottom. As I recovered from the momentary blast of wind and sand, I stood and tried to dust off the sand, but my sweat held the sand like glue. I resumed my trek up the dune.

After what seemed like hours in real time, I reached a point where I could see a palm frond waving in the sky just beyond the top of the dune. The thought of shade and possibly water filled me with new energy, and I quickened my pace. At the top, exhausted, I found the shade and rest I craved beneath a palm tree whose branch had beckoned me upward. A pitcher of cool water awaited my eager lips and I slowly drank the small portion that had been allotted me. For a short time, I thought my quest was over; yet, I asked myself "for what purpose?" Perhaps it was the strain I needed to overcome, to prove to myself I could accomplish something I might once have thought impossible. But that was too similar to what I had endured in the canyon. I dismissed the thought. I closed my eyes in the hope I would be whisked back to the cocoon to discuss this adventure with my other self. Nothing happened. I waited longer with my head bowed and my eyes closed. Still, nothing happened.

With encroaching despair, I opened my eyes and saw in the distance two separate, but seemingly identical oases. Blinking and shaking my head to be certain of what I saw, I was amazed that I had missed seeing them before. Perhaps, I reassured myself, they weren't there before. My despair was washed away by the sense of new commitment. Now the time had come for a true choice. I stood, shielded my eyes from the glare of the sun and searched the horizon and both sites for a clue. The distance to each oasis and between them looked nearly the same but traveling the total distance would be insurmountable. I knew I would have to choose one oasis over the other. I looked again and again, back and forth to discover any differences. The rising waves of heat off the dunes obscured a clear view, preventing me from pinpointing details. The heat was beginning once again to take its toll. Even standing still I could feel the heat searing away my energy ounce by ounce. However, doing nothing was once again not an option.

I stepped out from under the now withering palm branches, knowing my time of rest had come to an end and headed straight toward the two green refuges. The question that lay deep in my mind was whether either oasis was real. Perhaps one was a mirage, or even both. I dismissed the notion, at least in the hope that both might be real. My plan was to travel directly between them, stopping at intervals to examine them as clearly as I could until I was able to determine which oasis would be the better choice. The journey, though arduous, was not as difficult as the ascent up the dunes. I trekked on across the flat terrain, the sun fixed in a position above me. At a point, I assumed equal distance from each oasis, I stopped to again survey the landscape. Looking closely at the trees and configuration of the mounds of sand, I perceived a slight difference at the base of one tree in the oasis to the right. The sand appeared to rise to a ridge around the base of a tree, while at the base of the corresponding tree in the other oasis, the sand sank away. It was a negligible difference, but a difference none-the-less. My assumption was that if the sand at the base of one tree slipped away, there might be something more to see in the hollow beneath the tree. I made the decision to proceed toward the oasis to the left.

It didn't take very long for me to reach the oasis and happily I could see crystal blue water shimmering in the sand beyond the base of the tree. Was it the correct decision? I hoped so! My feet glided across the sand, barely sinking into the granular surface. Faster and faster until I reached the oasis, sinking to the ground and plunging my face into the inviting water. I had a total disregard for the purity of the water; I simply wanted and needed water. No sooner had my face submerged beneath the surface of the cool water, I found myself back in the cocoon.

"You look like hell," he said. "No, you look like you've been to hell. You're dripping wet and your skin is burned. Are you all right?"

I wasn't certain how to answer. "I'm exhausted. I don't feel much of anything except tired."

"Lay down and quietly rest. We can talk after it's gone."

"Gone? What's gone?" As I spoke, I felt a coolness come over me; my body and clothes dried as sweat evaporated and the redness of my skin faded. The pain I felt throughout my body subsided.

"Feel better?" he asked.

"Yes. What just happened?"

"What you endured that affected your body has left you and returned to its origin." He paused. "You did well. I felt our decisiveness and your commitment to move forward. You thought through the situation and decided what was best, even though there were unknowns along the way."

"I did good?"

"You did very well."

"But what about you? You don't look like you experienced anything at all."

"Remember, mine is a spiritual journey, not a physical one. You held on to faith in yourself and your ability to make decisions and that sustained me. Now rest."

Again, the routine of drowsiness repeated itself but before I completely drifted off to sleep, I felt his presence enter me.

CHAPTER EIGHT: PATHWAY THROUGH THE GARDEN

One of the lessons I learned, without leaving the cocoon, was the value of rest. In my often, hectic world, I had forgotten to take time for myself. As I awoke, I recalled those infrequent days of rest; remembering the day I had stepped into the glass. This was the first time I had looked back, not in any attempt to try to return, no longing for what had been, just a moment of remembrance as I stirred from sleep. I had set that day aside for a few domestic chores, but mostly for relaxation. I knew now those days would need to be more intentional, more frequent.

As I sat up, I saw my other self sitting, head bowed, deep in thought.

"Is there a problem?" I asked. He raised his head.

"No. I was just thinking about your thoughts on rest."

"Really? You know what I'm thinking? That's rather frightening."

"It's not what you might think, wrong choice of words. Remember, I am a part of you, so your thoughts come to me as well."

I stood up about to protest, when he raised a hand to stop me.

"I'm not a judge. You have the right to think whatever you wish. My purpose is to help guide your thoughts to action, positive action. You must not forget that I am that spark of God within you."

"My conscience?"

"That's one way to look at it; but there is far more. You have the free will to decide your own actions, but I am a subtle guide who holds the scale to weigh your options for you. This entire experience is to help you understand how to make better decisions in your life by listening to yourself."

"But why now? Why not when I was younger and had more life ahead of me?"

"I am not the one to choose the 'when.' It is best if you don't dwell on it. Perhaps later there will be a time and place to delve into the 'why.' For now, it's time to leave. The opening has begun to appear."

I held back, hesitant to take the steps to the outer rim of the cocoon. The last few experiences had each time brought me to the edge of exhaustion, and I was not anxious to repeat that feeling of fatigue. Still, I knew I had to take those meager steps, to move out of the comfort of the cocoon and into the solitary realm of new experience.

"Go on," my other self urged me. "I'll be there with you." His words were encouragement enough and I walked toward the opening and began the next chapter of uncertainty. Ever since my first experience in the valley when I opened my eyes to find where I had been brought, I found within me a caution, a "wait and see" attitude. I never knew what to expect, and this time was no different. I stood in the midst of a never-ending garden; a patchwork quilt of colors. The fragrances bombarded my sense of smell with a myriad of comforting aromas.

Should I touch the flowers? Should I pick one? Did I dare move? Shades of red, yellow, purple and blue abounded, interspersed with whites. Lavenders, roses, lilies, carnations, hyacinths, lilacs, daffodils and others I didn't recognize at all. It seemed as though all the seasons had blossomed at once, bringing together plants from across the globe into one spectacular garden arena. Appearing to be random, the path where I stood stretched out and disappeared, its rambling trail hidden by the blooms, gave me reason to believe there was an intentionality about the garden.

I began to slowly walk, following the path. Memories of my grandmother's rock garden flooded my mind, overwhelming me with feelings of loss. None of the other scenes had evoked any solid memories from my past, but here I felt drawn back in time to gardens, funerals and parties. There was a mix of feelings, happy and sad, jumbled together in my head and heart. I stopped walking, uncertain whether to go on or just remain standing, admiring the beauty that surrounded me. Would this garden be a repeat of one of my previous experiences? Would the flower disintegrate in my hand? Reaching out, I picked a flower, a lilac blossom, brought it to my face, closed my eyes as I forced the deep burgundy flower around my nose and inhaled a deep breath. The fragrance permeated my very being, sending a rush of overwhelming joy throughout me. I opened my eyes. The blossom had neither disintegrated nor had the spot where the blossom had once been attached, replicate that which had been removed.

Why was this so different from the others, I wondered. I resumed my walk, all the while taking periodic sniffs of the lilac blossom. I was so happy I hadn't noticed the dark clouds that had built up, hiding the blue sky and slowly masking the sun's rays. Lightning flashed in a circle around me, ringing the garden with streaks of white from sky to ground forming a series of celestial fence posts. More and more lightning burst and claps of earth-shaking thunder isolated me from the fringes of the garden and beyond. I saw no place to hide, no escape from the flashing light and thunderous roar from above.

When the sun's rays had been totally blocked from view and the garden veiled in near nighttime darkness, a stillness, a pause interceded, then the rains began. Torrential rains cascaded down from above, washing away the colors of the flowers, and carrying away the soothing fragrances. I watched in amazement believing I was seeing a great work of art scrubbed off the canvas by some solvent, leaving only a blank and hollow reminder of what had once been. The rain slowed from torrent to sprinkle. I wiped away the beads of water from my face, shook the rain out of the hair, standing transfixed by the sight of a once flourishing garden reduced to a field of dull gray and twisted undergrowth. The loss I had felt from memories of flowers from my youth was replaced by a more consuming deprivation of all things beautiful. I collapsed to the ground, tears flowing down my cheeks. I had been reduced to a sullen, broken man. Had it not been for a single shaft of sunlight piercing the clouds, I might had been left there a mass of human depression.

That single ray of light split the clouds, opening them more and more to the blue sky above. The ray became a veil of light, sweeping across the garden restoring it to life. I stood, watching as the dried, lifeless plants were brought back to life. What had been before the rains, to my amazement returned. Flowers blossomed everywhere. I breathed in fresh, fragrant air and my joy returned. At that instant, a sudden flash of lightning momentarily blinded me, and I found I had been returned to the cocoon. I stood with my other self smiling at me.

"What are you thinking?" he asked.

"I thought you knew what I thought."

"I want you to tell me out loud so you can hear it yourself."

"I felt joy. I remembered my grandmother's garden, parties, funerals too."

"How did you feel when it was all washed away?"

"A little like a child who built a sandcastle on the beach only to have it washed away by a wave. Gone forever."

"But you still have the memories."

"Yes, I do."

"Memories," he said, "are our link to the past and a door to our identity. What do you believe the experience was all about?"

I paused, contemplating the experience. "I suppose...." I halted while I thought more deeply about what had happened. "I suppose, it was to remind me that my past is never forgotten, it's inside of me. It has shaped me. But I don't understand why it was all washed away and then came back. Was it meant to be a resurrection or reincarnation?"

"Not at all. Life is filled with color, in the world around us and within me; but, sometimes we lose sight of those colors and the world turns gray. Faith and hope carry us through the gray and return us to the color. It's all part of the everyday cycle of life. While some people remain trapped in the gray, colorless world, we can be there to help re-color their world."

"I understand that. Yet, in every experience I have been alone, except having you with me, so where are all the others I might be able to help?"

"That question will be answered soon enough."

"Here?'

"Here and back there."

"I don't feel like I need to rest. Even though I felt remorse for the loss, it went away when the sunlight restored everything in the garden. Can I go on to the next chapter now?" He smiled. "That's not up to you or me. We'll just have to wait and see. Sit down and see what happens next."

Chapter Nine: Pathway Through the Mountain Cave

Waiting can be as trying as attempting to endure the difficulties of life's traumas. Just sitting in silence, we waited. Possibly it was as long as half an hour, or perhaps as short as a few minutes, I will never know. At last the cocoon's passageway revealed itself. I stood and began to walk toward the opening when I felt a hand on my shoulder.

"Wait," he said. "This one we do together."

I stood motionless as I felt him enter me. As one we left the cocoon. When I arrived at my point of entry, two thoughts crossed my mind: why were we to be together this time? And, what was I supposed to do standing on the edge of a mountain cliff? Instinctively I moved away from the edge, as close to the mountain face as possible. I took a deep breath then began to take stock in the situation.

This was the first time my attire had changed. Instead of the t-shirt, jeans and shoes from the house, now I wore a padded jacket over my shirt and heavy hiking boots. Even my jeans were made of a thicker canvas-like material. Over my shoulder was slung a backpack, which after a quick examination revealed a flashlight, rope, miner's helmet and other items I assumed were necessary for climbing. I looked up the steep rocky face of the mountain, then down the precipice behind me. Was I to go up or down? Then I saw the black hole in the side of the mountain—a cave. Those were spelunking supplies in the backpack. I was not to go up or down the mountain, but into it. A wave of fear rose within me as I stood motionless. Darkness had never been my friend; I had always much preferred light where I could see what was happening around me. At that moment I understood why my other self was with me. I would need all the strength I could muster to overcome the challenge and my fears.

With a long breath, I put the helmet on my head, turned on its light and walked to the cave entrance, out of the daylight into the mountain's inner darkness. My only experience with caves was in commercial, tourist attractions that moved people along a prescribed, lighted pathway. Now I walked on uncharted ground, peppered with random stones, walls that in one instance surged toward me, closing in on me like thick fog, while at other times receding, opening to wide expansive cavities. Once I had my bearings, was sure of my footing, the fears momentarily subsided and I began to admire the beauty of that subterranean world.

Walls sometimes flickered as the beam of my helmet light struck crystals in the cave walls. As I walked along, I found myself listening to the trickle of water: water dropping from the ceiling, water cascading down walls and tumbling along at my feet as I descended further into the cave. Stalactites clung to the ceiling like choruses of mineral icicles, while stalagmites grew beneath them, another gathering of choristers standing erect in solemn procession. The hues of the rock walls changed with each turn, exposed by the millennia of erosion from seeping rains from above.

At times the ground was slippery, and I had to carefully maneuver around ledges that had been created by fallen ceiling stones. There were places where I had to remove the backpack to be able to squeeze through narrow passages, while in other places I had to resort to crawling on hands and knees to move from one chamber to another. Entering upon what became the largest chamber, I sat to decide my next course of action. Rest was a welcome diversion from the constant calculation of every movement. Ahead of me opened four passages. Time for a decision!

I decided to follow the flow of water, hoping that it would ultimately lead me out of the mountain. That was at least the plan. Rested and committed to my choice of passages, I moved on. The descent became steeper and several times I lost my footing and slid along the smooth rock surface until I could catch myself, stopping my forward progress. It wasn't until after several more unfortunate slips that I realized the flashlight had fallen out of the backpack and had been lost somewhere in the maze behind me. I had been using the helmet light and fortunately that light continued to illuminate my way. I kept hearing a voice in my head, saying, "Keep going. Keep going." I did just that, at least until I reached a steep drop off. The stream I had been following suddenly cascaded over a cliff to a pool below. Another choice had to be made.

I never considered retracing my steps, but now I wondered if that was a choice I should re-evaluate. I decided it wasn't feasible. I needed to move forward, not backwards. A quick glance around the summit of the falls revealed several substantial pieces of the walls that had come loose and now rested on the cave floor. Removing the backpack, I took out the rope, looped it around the largest of the stones and threw the other end of the rope over the falls, the end of the rope splashing into the water below. The distance down was not extreme, but too far to jump, and uncertain of what might lie beneath the surface of the water, climbing down the rope was my best choice. I could see exposed ground around the edges of the pool, and the continuation of the stream emptying into the darkness beyond.

Wearing the gloves from the backpack I prepared for the descent. I had never done anything like it before, but knew if I should fall, the distance was not so great that I would probably survive. I remembered that my other self had once said no one ever dies, but he didn't say anything about cuts, bruises and broken bones. It seemed that every episode was a totally new experience and I wondered how this one would end; and when it would end. Tightly gripping the rope, I started down. My self-assurance was soon shattered when I lost my grip and fell feet-first into the pool of cold water at the base of the falls. To my surprise and delight, the water was only waist deep. I happily made my way to the shoreline, pulled myself up onto a slab of rock and there contemplated what to do next. My boots had filled with water, so I removed them, poured out the water and set them down beside me. I took off my socks, wrung out what water I could, and then put them back on the feet.

There was only one passageway out of the cavern, and I stepped away from the pool to shine my light down the narrow earthen hallway. It was then my helmet light flickered and went out. I stood there in the darkness, confused and perplexed: no light, no boots, no rope and a backpack of supplies I had left up on the ledge above the waterfall. The chill of the water-soaked pant legs and socks, coupled with my resurfaced fear of darkness, sent shudders through me. Time for another decision.

In that moment I left like a small child left in the dark, waiting for someone to rescue them and lead them to safety. Who was my rescuer and where were they? At that point, for the first time in as long as I could remember, I got down on my knees and prayed for help. I felt totally disconnected, abandoned and alone. Perhaps it was the darkness which weighed on me like a black fog; perhaps it was the sense of loneliness that had been accumulating with each experience. Where was my other self? He said he would be with me!

Prayer was never easy for me; it seemed so abstract, unrelatable to the moment. But I prayed just the same. I prayed to be free of the darkness and the unknowing of that hollow in the ground. I prayed for a guiding light to lead me safely out of the murky, monstrous belly of the mountain. As I prayed, I crawled, feeling the stream as my guide; always inching along the stony surface. I crawled because I felt less likely to injure my head against the cave wall or lose my footing and fall.

I crawled one hand and foot after another, following the twists and turns of the tunnel; each twist and turn testing my endurance and perseverance. I whispered over and over the prayer for the help that would lead me to safety. I raised my head and could see a dim light in the distance, faintly intruding on the darkness that had engulfed me. I dared not quicken my pace for fear of injury, but in reality, I probably did. The light, once a dim spark in the distance now grew brighter with each approaching crawl. I could see it was an opening to the outside world, its light illuminating enough of the cave, so I could stand and walk the remaining span between captivity and freedom.

At last I stood in the open, breathing deeply of the fresh air, inhaling it as if it was giving me my life back. Behind me lay a dark past, now I stood in the future light. I looked at my hands, bloodied from the trek, my feet, worn through the sock and bloodied as well; my pants and shirt tattered. I was so happy to be out of the cave I didn't even remember how any of the cuts and bruises happened. It didn't matter. Another deep breath in, eyes closed, and I was swept back to the cocoon.

I lay there, my cuts and bruises healing before my eyes, my clothes slowly restored, but my other self was nowhere to be seen. Exhausted, I closed my eyes and fell into a deep sleep. Sometime during that recuperative nap, we separated, and it was his voice that awakened me.

"What?" I mumbled.

"We should talk," he said.

"Yes." I stirred myself enough to sit up. "I thought you were going to be with me? Where were you?" I became angry at what appeared to be a broken trust between us. "I can't keep going on like this, alone, facing obstacles I can't overcome."

"But you did overcome it."

"I was cut, bruised, on the verge of giving up. I hate the dark and you left me there in that cave."

"You may have been on the verge of giving up, but you didn't" As my voice had escalated, his calm tones offset my anger. "I was with you every moment."

"Don't give me that crap! None of this is getting me anywhere. I'm done with it. I want out!"

"I'm sorry to hear you say that, but it's not for you, or me, to decide."

"What is for me to decide?"

"Everything you have: scaling the canyon wall, choosing the right oasis, crawling your way out of the cave, praying. You made those choices."

"And there'll be more, I suppose. But why? And where have you been?"

There was a long pause as we both awkwardly stared at each other. It was looking in the mirror at the end of a long day trying to assess the day's experiences. He spoke first. "I was with you this last time, speaking to you the entire time. It was my voice you heard. It was me helping you make the tough decisions. I was the one who heard your prayers."

"But I didn't hear anything. I remember thinking I could use all your help as I faced that cave entrance, but you never said a word."

"I didn't need to. While I'm within you, we are one. I don't need to speak as you might imagine. You feel my thoughts, you know I'm there."

"Sometimes I think a little more would help. I turned my face away and sat in the middle of the cocoon with my back to him.

"Why do you think you decided to crawl out of the cave instead of walking out? Why do you think you followed that streambed?"

"Those were all logical, reasonable things to do."

"Yes, they were." He came around and squatted in front of me. "Some of that you've learned through experience. Some of it is just part of who you are. I'm that part of you. I helped guide your hand beside the water. I kept your head down low so it wouldn't hit the cave ceiling. I kept fueling your energy to keep you going. I heard your prayers. I've always been with you, you just didn't know it, now you do."

"Now I do." I reluctantly agreed. There was another long silence. We sat while the silence continued. A sliver of light appeared behind him and I knew it was time to leave once more.

"Remember, no matter what, I'm with you; whether within you or in spirit." I stood and stepped through the opening in the cocoon wall, leaving my other self behind.

CHAPTER TEN: PATHWAY THROUGH THE ISLAND

When my eyes were able to adjust to the bright light, I found myself on a sandy beach. The blue waters sparkled in the sunlight as small waves, nothing more than over-excited ripples, gently rolled onto the sand. It was time for an inspection tour. I removed my shoes and socks, walked barefoot to the water's edge and dipped my hands into the water, scooping up enough to taste. Saltwater! I was on the shoreline of an ocean. I didn't know which ocean it was; it didn't matter since it probably wasn't any known ocean at all. Next the shoreline. In either direction the sandy beach swept off inland. I was either standing on a promontory or an island. Beyond the beach sand, a tangle of brush and trees, a lush interior that beckoned me to explore; but first, a walk along the beach to determine the size and scope of the land mass. I left my shoes and socks as markers on the beach and headed off in what might have been north, but I really wasn't certain.

I walked and walked along the shoreline, crossing a freshwater creek that flowed down from what I later discovered was a knoll in the interior. Next came rocks, jutting up out of the sand. I climbed to the top, scanning the horizon for any sign of other land, but there was none to be seen. I dashed over the rocks and to the other side where I could see that the shoreline continued off to my right. I continued to follow the sandy pathway between the water and the vegetation until I arrived back at the point where I had left my shoes and socks. How far I had walked was difficult to tell; however, my legs ached from the exploration. My feet burned from the sand and periodically I had stepped into the water to cool and comfort them. Now that I was back at my point of origin, I decided to assess the situation.

I knew I was on an island. I thought of all those proverbial dilemmas: Who would you want to be stranded with on a deserted island? What book would you bring? What one item would you bring along with you? They were all questions that had no concrete answers. People often think of great religious or notable individuals from history as their companion on a deserted island; but what about the total stranger with whom to spend long hours revealing life's stories? What book? Perhaps a dictionary or atlas. So many choices, none of them fully adequate; none of them to solve the problem of being stranded and alone.

Having decided I would have brought along a boat and motor to get off the island, and that modern electronics didn't count as a remedy for an age-old question, I ventured to the interior of the island. Slipping on my socks and shoes for protection against the unknown, I stepped off the sand into the underbrush. My pathway was a circuitous one as I avoided rocks, trees and vines. I hoped I was inching ever closer to the center but was uncertain since I had made so many twists and turns. My view of the shoreline and the ocean was obscured by tall grasses, bushes and trees. I wondered if at any moment I would burst through back on the beach and have to start all over once again. The heat of the day began to have an impact on my energy level. While it wasn't as severe as my trek through the desert heat, it was none-the-less, enough to turn my clothes into soaking sweat sponges.

A steady upward incline greeted me in a clearing. Surrounded by the near-jungle environment, I welcomed the open space. Walking was now easier, and while the sun was unobscured, the exertion was less, and the open area was a relief from the battle with vines and sharp-edged, stiff foliage. I trudged onward up the hill until I reached the summit. From that vantage point I could see the rocky outcroppings on one side of the island and just behind me the source of the freshwater stream I had crossed on the beach. The spring of clear waster bubbled up from a cleft in the exposed rock, trickling down the hillside in a well-worn streambed, disappearing into the underbrush.

Another oasis, I thought to myself. Perhaps a refreshing drink would send me back to the cocoon as had my previous experience in the desert. I bent down, cupped my hands together, dipped them in the water, then took a slow drink of the cool water. It quenched my thirst, but not enough, so I took another drink and then a third. I found myself still standing next to the water. A wave of exhaustion overtook me, and I decided to move from the hard rock seat I had taken, to the soft ground beside the rock. There I fell asleep.

When I awoke, I was back in the cocoon. I stood and looked around, but my other self was nowhere to be seen. A shudder of panic overtook me at being alone in the cocoon. "Calm down," a familiar voice said. I turned and was face-to-face with my other self. My shudder of panic had also been his moment of release.

"I'm getting tired of walking in circles," I said. "Time after time, I'm left to make all these decisions, and then, like a miracle, or wave of a magic wand, a solution, or an oasis appears, and the experience is over." My frustration was mounting. "Why? Every time I'm backed into a corner 'poof' some random resolution brings me back here. When is it going to be over? I'm tired; the sleep doesn't seem to restore my strength. Enough is enough!" I sat exasperated by the ongoing, seemingly endless sequence of experiences that appeared to have no purpose.

He circled around me, then spoke in that gentle tone I had come to know so well. "I've told you before, there is no way of knowing how many experiences you will have to endure. We've been over this before."

"But ...." He silenced me with a raised hand.

"Each experience has a purpose. What did you learn this time?"

"I don't know."

"Think."

I paused. "Don't get stuck alone on a deserted island." He didn't laugh, not even a smile. Another pause. "There's a solution to every dilemma."

"Close. Every situation has its own oasis. It may come to you. You may have to search for it, but it's there. An oasis isn't just a palm tree, ladder, water spring, it's an answer to a problem. Life requires us to explore, to seek out the oasis of our dreams, of our hopes, of change, or our new life. You have been finding each oasis and in so doing you have grown stronger. At some point you will have all the strength you need, and you will leave the cocoon and go home."

Home was where I really wanted to be. His words settled in like wisdom to be absorbed and applied. I sat down, laid back and fell sleep. There we both rested, side-by-side, together, but apart for now.

CHAPTER ELEVEN: PATHWAY THROUGH THE SWAMP

I was startled out of a sound sleep by his hands shaking my shoulder. "The gateway has opened," he said. There it was, the wall of the cocoon parted by some unseen force, beckoning me once again to pass through it. "Go now. You have to hurry." I stood, shook off the last vestiges of sleep and walked to the opening.

"What about you?" I asked.

"This time I have to stay. Go." His hands motioned me forward to the opening. I stepped through the curtain of light and found myself knee-deep in water. Billowing clouds of white and gray marched across the sky above, sometimes blotting out the sun and other times opening up for the sun to cast its rays of light on me. The affect was like a strobe light, a rolling sequence of alternating light and dark, like scenes from a movie told in rapid motion.

I soon realized I was standing in the midst of a vast swamp. Like some primordial landscape caught in the vice-grip of interrupted time. The water was warm, but not hot, coated with a growth of algae. The air had a foul smell to it of rot. Shooting up from the water, standing like pillars, were barbless trees, their bleached wood solemn reminders of a life once lived. A few trees, with branches pointing upward, looked like hands with fingers crying out as they reached up trying to escape the swampy slime. Stubby green bushes populated the swamp showing off life in the midst of an otherwise desolate surrounding. I imagined prehistoric creatures roaming the swamp, searching for food, both plant and animal.

There was an eerie silence about the swamp, not one of lifelessness, but of life deserted. It was as if all life had fled the swamp in dread, sensing an impending danger. That same feeling came over me. I had not felt it before, not in the desert, nor in the cave. Even the clouds moving across the dome of the sky seemed to exude foreboding. Periods of bright light became infrequent as the clouds settled together into a gray blanket across the sky.

While there were groves of dead trees standing together like families caught in death's grip, there were also large open areas of algae covered water. The same scene greeted me no matter where I looked, but I decided I couldn't just stand where I had stood since arriving. I wiggled one shoe then the other; my shoes were caught in the mud, but not so securely that they were immobile. Gradually I loosened one foot and took a step, then the other. Each time I disturbed the water, the stench increased, rising up enflaming my nostrils. I decided to make my way toward a small grove of dead trees and green bushes hoping the ground there would be more stable.

It turned out to be a good choice. The ground beneath the water rose up to half the depth from where I had begun. Grasping one of the tree trunks, I pulled myself up between the trees. There I stood, only ankle deep in water, feeling a sense of security from the swamp itself. The green leaves on the bushes gave life to the area and I felt protected from the swamp itself. My feeling of security would not last.

In the distance I saw the algae moving up and down as if the water beneath it was breathing. The movement of the algae shifted to one side and moved along a ridge of green bushes, then back into the open water. I saw nothing but the movement of the surface. The algae provided an excellent shield to what moved below it. Perhaps I had been transported to some prehistoric locale where terrible beasts and hidden denizens of the deep lurked waiting to strike. Turning over all the different scenarios in my mind. I determined that I might have to defend myself from whatever occupied the swamp.

The trees where I stood, were close enough together that I could use them like a ladder, and a climbed out of the water and up to what I thought might be a safe distance. The movement in the water made a rapid turn and began circling the cluster of trees. My heart began to beat faster and faster, my breathing became more intense. No longer did I notice the smell of the swamp. A dead branch, one of the last vestiges of how the tree had held up its beauty, was within my reach. I lunged for it, tightly gripped the aged, brittle wood, and broke it loose from its parent trunk. The circles of rippling water tightened around my tree and bush fortress; but now I had a weapon to defend myself if necessary.

As the ripples grew in size, the algae began to separate, and I could see the dark form of the creature who inhabited the swamp. It didn't swim like a snake, back and forth, but more like a fish or reptile. It circled and circled, faster and faster, churning the algae into a frenzied mixture of green bobbing up and down, pushed by the ripples away from my island fortress. The black creature who exposed its back occasionally as it swam, seemed more agitated as it circled.

Dare I strike at it with my spear? Such an attempt might incur its wrath with the creature striking back in self-defense, leaving my life in jeopardy. Suddenly the movement in the water stopped. At that point I had no sense of where the beast might be. I drew myself higher into the trees seeking the protection of distance. I mused that the creature was water-bound and therefore I was out of reach. The water below me began to churn with the beast's body stirring up the mud from the bottom of the swamp. It was then I realized it was digging a channel in the mud to get closer to the base of the trees. I watched in terror from my refuge, as the creature reached the base of the tree and proceeded to whip up the muddy waters into a foaming cauldron of seething stench. Just then I heard a crack from the dead tree that was my sanctuary and I fell backwards into the swampy water, still holding onto the tree.

I bolted to my feet, shook off the water, opened my eyes and found myself back in the cocoon with my other self-smiling at me.

"What are you smiling about? I just went through another hell, terrorized by, I don't know what."

"That was me," he said.

"What? You've got to be kidding me. What was that all about? You said you had to stay here. You lied to me."

"It was a test."

"A test," I shouted. It was the first time I had raised my voice at him. "Being tested is one thing, being terrified is another. A test is when you sit and answer questions. That was no test, it was a horror story come to life."

"A test is also finding out how far your limits will stretch before...."

"Before the tree breaks and you get eaten by some prehistoric monster?"

"Not at all. Believe me I wasn't going to eat you."

"I didn't know that."

"No, you didn't, that was intentional. Up until now you have been alone on all your tests. This time you faced an opponent outside of yourself. Your fear was a natural reaction to the situation. We learn fear, but we also learn how to handle it—or at least we should." He paused. "What were you afraid of?"

"You!"

"No, not me. You didn't know it was me."

"That thing in the water. I couldn't figure out what it was."

"You were afraid of what you didn't understand. Every other time, it was the unknown that forced you to decide. But in each of those decisions, there was nothing that stood in your way except your own lack of determination. You fought through to reach the end. In the cave you faced your own fear of the dark, but with my help we succeeded. In the swamp it wasn't only your fear, but an adversary you had to overcome. That adversary wasn't some denizen of the deep, but your lack of knowledge and understanding of it."

"But it just ended with the tree breaking off and me falling."

"Did it?" he asked. "Think back and tell me what you remember."

I closed my eyes attempting to recall all that had led up to the tree breaking and my fall into the swamp water. "The water got all foamy and the creature, you, started up out of the water. I raised my spear, pushed with one foot against the other tree for support, and when I did the tree, I was in broke off. As I started to fall, I threw the spear." I paused. "I threw the spear at you as you came out of the water." I opened my eyes and there he was still smiling at me. "Will you stop smiling. What does that mean? I defended myself. Anything more than that?"

"You defended yourself against both what frightened you and what you didn't understand. While a spear is not really the answer, it represented a tool, reaching out to challenge fear and ignorance."

"Then we should battle for what we believe?"

"In a way, but not with weapons, but with wisdom. The spear was all you had to defend yourself, and you needed to do just that, defend yourself. The question was whether or not you would defend yourself at all, and you did. You used your knowledge and instinct for self-preservation to overcome an unknown obstacle. Life is filled with obstacles, as you're learning, but it isn't about weapons of defense, but the wisdom of defense that matters."

"I need to think about that. By the way, did I hit you?"

"What?"

"With the spear. Did I hit you?

"Does it matter?"

There was no need for an answer to the question. Sleep came as easily as it had every time before. In that time of almost sleep, I felt his presence enter me once more.

CHAPTER TWELVE: PATHWAY THROUGH THE WATERS

Part I: The River

When I awoke, I found myself seated on a wet rock ledge inside a mountain whose rock center had been chiseled out by raging waters. I was surprised to find myself there, not having awakened in the cocoon and then coaxed out through the opening that always appeared. I quickly dismissed the mechanics and sequences that moved me to where I was, instead choosing to determine the reality of my present circumstances.

The cave roared with rushing water, flowing from a large opening high above me, into the cave. The spray of the cold clear water made the interior of the cave glisten, each drop of water clinging to the rock walls sparkling like dew drops in the morning sun. Cracks and clefts in the walls breached the mountain allowing light to filter in from the outside, illuminating the cave. The steel-blue water led me to believe that I might be at the origin of a river; a truth I would soon discover. The icy water found its beginning in a glacier high on the mountain. As the icy mass inched its way down the peak and melted, it had, millennia ago, ruptured the mountain rock, gradually honing out first a narrow passage and now the cave.

I felt compelled to follow the flow of the water down through the stone tunnel it had carved, so began a very slow and slippery descent. The action of the water had worn away a wider berth than the river now needed, so there was room to navigate down inside the mountain. When I arrived at a point where the water sank deep into a crevasse, I had to search for an alternative route. I found one, long unused by the torrents of water, and so made my escape from inside the peak to the sundrenched, dry land outside.

Above me rose the apex of the mountain range, whitecapped and majestic. Below me, a lush green valley. I could hear waterfalling to the earth below, but it was out of sight. The climb down was not as arduous as other climbs I had made, and I smiled with the ease of this adventure. The cave had not been dark, the pathway down the mountain easily discernable amid the grasses and brush. I wondered if everything that had come before was but a prelude to this and what more was to come.

When I finally reached the valley, I turned and looked back at the scale of the mountain I had just descended. Its distant whitecapped peak rose up out of the valley beside other mountains, a majestic brotherhood of old men with white hair and beards guarding the distant lands beyond them. I could now see where the water surged out of the rockface, falling to the grassy plain below. The deep blue water, clear as crystal, flowed on near me, in first a straight course and then a meandering, ever widening stream.

I walked along beside the stream, joined as it was by other mountain streams that had also escaped from mountaintops, growing in volume the further it traveled through the valley. When a second, even larger stream merged with it, it became a river deep and wide. I marveled at how the water gently flowed along, dropping by inches the water quickening its pace as it continued on. I discovered a deserted raft. It was then I wondered if this had all been perfectly planned for me; but then, the other experiences had been set in motion by a force far beyond my understanding. I thought of my other self, asking myself where he might be. Was he still within me? Was he in some sphere where he endured the spiritual beside my physical journey? I had no way of knowing.

Since each journey had led to some climatic ending, I questioned where this one might lead. The idyllic surroundings, the ease of movement lulled me into a sense of calm. Perhaps this was some Eden, and my tests were over, having achieved my goals; this being a reward for work well done. I found that hard to accept, pushed the raft out into the water and began a gradual, slow ride down the stream.

On the raft were an oar, some rope looped around one of the logs, presumably for holding on, and a small anchor tied by rope to the raft. As I rode along the water on the raft, the mountains passed in silent review, soon becoming a landscape not of mountains but high hills. Forests appeared with trees encroaching along the riverbanks, sometimes having been loosened from their earthen moorings and set adrift. The river again quickened its flow and the raft bobbed in the waves as the water passed over the uneven riverbed. The primitive raft, no more than logs lashed together, maneuvered the waters well, and with the use of the oar I was able to keep from getting lodged in some cove, on a sandbar or rocks.

For the most part, the ride was uneventful, but as the river narrowed to a channel between steep banks and stone barriers protruded from beneath the surface of the water, the journey became instantly more hazardous. While at one point the raft had merely bobbed up and down as waves crested as it passed over unseen anomalies on the bottom riverbed, now the water foamed with turbulence. The raft, drawn by the power of the water, was pulled along faster and faster, weaving from one side of the river then thrust to the opposite side skirting around outcroppings not yet worn down by the water's continual flow. I soon realized the value of holding on to the rope with one hand to stabilize myself and keep the anchor and oar secure with my other hand.

As the raft was both pulled along and thrust about, my increasingly precarious predicament became obvious. With one sudden upward force as the water swirled around then over a rock ledge, the raft was thrown airborne. I lost my grip, both on the oar, anchor and the rope loop and found myself sinking below the surface of the water. I awaited my return to the cocoon, but it didn't come. Struggling to the surface, gasping for air, I managed to climb out onto the rocks that had sent me backwards into the water. Ahead of me the raft danced about in the chaotic waters, held stationary by the anchor lodged firmly between two rocks. With a sigh of relief that all was not totally lost and with water pounding at my back forcing me ever closer to catapulting off the rock and back at the mercy of the raging river, I jumped forward, caught the anchor rope and pulled myself onto the raft.

"Any time now," I shouted out loud to a world that had no ears to hear. "If this was not the end of the journey, what comes next," I asked. A momentary lapse into a state of self-pity ended when I realized I had to break loose from the anchor to continue my journey.

Part II: The Waterfall

The raft held firmly together, continually yanking at the anchor rope. When each new surge of water, the strain on the rope increased. The force of the water kept the raft wobbling in the water while it remained tethered to the anchor which was proudly fulfilling its intended purpose. I sat on the raft, maintaining my grip on the rope that was looped around one log, my stomach becoming queasier with each gyration of the raft. If I was going to survive on the water, I had to have a plan. The current was too swift to battle against it, either to get to shore or move upstream. At some point the rope attached to the anchor was going to snap and the raft would be once again at the mercy of the untamed waters.

I decided that my clothes were more of a hindrance than a help, wet as they were, their weight would make any swimming extremely difficult. I stripped down to my underwear, hoping I could avoid crashing against any jagged rocks and injuring myself. No sooner had I slipped my shirt over my head and tossed it aside, the rope attached to the anchor snapped, launching me and the raft downstream. I grabbed the loop, my lifeline and held on with both hands.

The ride became more violent with each passing moment; the trees on the shoreline becoming a green blur as the raft bounced and spun around in rapid succession. I had no control of the raft, feeling helpless as the flow of water increased as other tributaries merged with what had once been simply a glacier stream. As a child I had listened as little streams bubbled and seemed to whisper to the banks, but now this river raged and billowed for all the world to hear. The sound of the water kept rising reaching a near deafening pitch, and I realized I was headed directly toward a waterfall. I could see ahead of me not more water, but the open expanse of blue sky. My only hope was that the waterfall was not very high, a hope soon toppled as the raft and I flew out of the water and into open air, beginning the long descent.

I never did see how far it was to the bottom of the cataract for my grip on the rope released and I found myself inundated by falling water. It is said when you're facing death, your life flashes before your eyes. It did. In bursts of milliseconds the story of my life was played out in my head. I saw myself playing in winter's snows and kite flying in open summer fields. I saw a parade of Christmas trees, heard voices singing joyous carols. I saw family members, long passed gone, and pets that had once been my companions. I saw flowered fields and desolate cemeteries. I saw classrooms, schoolmates, some life-long friends and others who evolved into strangers. There were romances, serious and frivolous; years of work. I saw my house, built board-by-board, my lawn manicured to as close to perfection as I could make it. I felt joy and heartache, satisfaction and regret, relief and stress. Most of all, I felt relief that it was all over. Surely, I would rise up out of the water and into the cocoon.

Part III. The Sea

I hit the water below the falls with enormous force and was pushed below the surface by the overwhelming power and weight of the cascading water. There was no cocoon to save me, only the lightless well of sea. Had I more time to fill my lungs with a long breath of air in anticipation of the plunge, I might have felt more comfortable in knowing I could outlast my submersion; but, there had been only a quick breath nearly beaten out of me by the plunge into the water. Now I faced my survival, struggling to swim to the surface. I swam upward, out of the foaming water from the waterfall that mixed with the sea water, away from the churning downward push of the falls. Reaching the surface and light, I gasped for air. There I rested, out of the turbulence in the calm sea.

In the dim light of dusk, I could see no land; the cliffs, waterfall and all lands seemingly faded away in the distance as if they never existed. Once more I had been set adrift, not in a canyon nor a desert, but in some vast unending sea. There was enough light to be able to discern any objects that might be floating on the surface. Surprisingly the raft was not far off, intact and waiting for my arrival. I swam the short distance to the raft and when I put my hand on the logs to pull myself aboard, I realized my watch was gone, ripped off by the force of the unrelenting waterfall. A small loss. I then came to the realization that my underwear was also gone, and I was naked. A more important loss; however, in the middle of nowhere, all alone, modesty was irrelevant. I pulled myself onto the raft and truly rested for the first time since entering the rapids of the river.

What was to come next? When a person is all alone, there is much time to just think; to mull over the "what ifs" and the litany of possibilities of what might come next. Throughout the long ordeal, from my beginning in the valley and now adrift on an endless sea, I had to come to grips with my identity, my purpose, my future. I had become less self-conscious and more aware of my surroundings. My other self-had told me "no one dies" during these journeys, but I had been told other half-truths before, ploys to get me to examine myself. Perhaps while I had come close, but had not died prior to this, this was the end; the ultimate test where survival was not an option. Perhaps death is after all, the only option to living, the final purpose. I found no comfort in that thought;

however, I did recall the inner calm I felt while being cast down in the midst of the waterfall. For a few moments more I rested.

When I awoke, fully expecting to be in the cocoon, the raft was caught in a growing tumult. I was being bounced around in the waves and instinctively I latched on to the loop that had so successfully held me in place while maneuvering the river cataracts. I scanned the horizon in every direction but there was nothing to see, only the line where the sky met the water, forming a giant circle around me. I felt like I was in a fishbowl with my observer blocked from view by the canopy of sky. That thought had entered my mind several times before, but there was nothing I could do about it.

The water began to churn and swirl within the expansive circle. I was now caught in a whirlpool drawing me closer and closer to the center. I rowed the water with my hands to try to counter the current, to no avail. The current was moving faster, spiraling the raft closer toward an as yet unseen center. Waves prevented me from seeing where I was headed as I swirled in ever tightening circles, bobbing and spinning around at the same time. I kept a firm grip on the loop of rope, huddling down against the raft in hope of not being cast overboard. I talked out loud, I prayed, I cursed. My emotions were running the gamut, but no life flashing before my eyes. All I could see was water; water that splashed onto my face obscuring my sight.

I wiped away a face full of water. In the distance I caught a glimpse of a head bobbing up and down in the water. "Hey you," I yelled. I got up off my stomach and knelt on the raft. Again, I shouted: "Hey you, over here. Over here." There was no response. I thought it might be an illusion, a trick in the midst of my desperation to survive. I shouted again and waved my one free hand in the air.

The head turned in my direction and two hands went momentarily up in the air. I couldn't make out any features, the darkness encroaching more and more as the last vestiges of sunlight dispersed across the horizon. The head and hands then sank into the water as a wave mounted up between us obstructing my view. I began to stroke the water using both hands to move the raft faster with the current. Again, the head bobbed up out of the water. The closer I got to the mystery person, the more desperate the situation became. I could now see the center of the maelstrom. We were being drawn into a hole in the sea, an orifice syphoning off the sea and everything with it.

I was now close enough to my struggling companion, who was fighting against the current. "Let me help you," I shouted as I reached out my one free hand. There was no response. In that moment I decided we would either drown or survive together and I leapt from the raft as the waters sucked it into the abyss. A single stroke and I was able to put my arms around the unsuspecting person and together our fate was sealed as we followed the raft into the abyss. Rushing, thundering water was replaced by dark silence.

I sat up spitting water as I coughed in an attempt to clear my lungs. Gasping for a breath of clear air, I realized I was back in the safety of the cocoon. My harsh coughs awakened my other self who lay naked beside me. It seemed both of us had been through a tumultuous experience. He sat up and we stared at each other. Nudity had never been an issue for me, but in that moment, I felt embarrassed and vulnerable as never before. Looking at one's naked self in a mirror is one thing, but looking at your other naked self, is something else. Our nakedness caused us both to look away.

"Let's get dressed," I suggested. Our clothes were neatly folded in two identical piles; my watch resting on the top. We dressed, each of us putting on the same piece of clothing in an identical manner. When we had finished, we sat facing each other.

"Was that my rebirth?" I asked. "I've read about such things, seen movies. Have I just been reborn in some cosmic religious ceremony?"

"Not exactly," he answered back.

"Well, exactly what?" I pressed him further. "Was that you I tried to save?"

"Yes."

"In one moment, you're some hideous creature and the next a drowning man. What's it all mean?"

"It's all about you. Who you are on the inside?"

"You told me at the very beginning that while I went through this physical journey, you would be going through some abstract spiritual journey at the same time. So, what happened? Was that all a lie?"

"No. Let me explain." There was a pause. "In the beginning, we were separated. I felt all that you endured; but as the journey became more treacherous and you were gaining confidence, my role changed. Instead of being a part of you, I became your challenger. Your feelings, your thoughts, guided my actions."

"So, I couldn't win no matter what I did. If I decided to turn right, you knew that and would go left. That's not fair; its diabolical and unjust."

"Not exactly. The purpose was not only to anticipate your actions, but to press you to go further, to reach deeper within yourself; to think and feel in ways you never had. Each experience on the journey built on the one before it, culminating in this last one. You didn't know it was me floundering around in the water, but you chose to try to save me, even though the results would probably prove futile." He paused again. "What were you thinking on that raft when you saw me?"

"I don't know." I hesitated to think. "I guess, if I could survive, then you should too

"But when it became obvious you were going down into the abyss, you still reached out for me. What were you thinking?"

"No one should die alone." My response surprised me. "If there was the possibility of surviving, I wanted you to survive as well. If we were going to die, we would die together. You needed to know someone cared."

"What about the knowledge that in this series of events, no one dies?"

"It never crossed my mind."

"And what about just trying to save yourself?"

"You were more important to me. So, what does it all mean?"

"It means you care, you always did, but had never been challenged on it before."

"That's it? I have always cared. This all seems wasted effort. And being spit out of that black abyss into this cocoon was not a rebirth?"

"Not in the physical sense. You're still the same person you were before, but now you know yourself better. This entire process was meant to strip you naked...."

"Literally."

"Literally, of all the pretense and self-assumptions you had built up about yourself. You have been turned inside out. This is the real you, sitting here with me. What are you thinking?"

"I never would have known any of this, would I?" He interrupted. "You might have discovered some of it for yourself." I now understood. "I would have gone through life without the appreciation for the world around me and without ever knowing what I was capable of accomplishing." I stood and walked away from my other self. "You knew all this, didn't you?"

"Yes. I am you, after all."

"It's like you've been hiding all my life. Sleeping, just waiting to awaken, or be awakened."

"That's true. For many people the other self never awakens, they never find their sacred center and therefore lead an incomplete life. Your life is now complete; not ended, just beginning."

"What happens next?" I asked. He stood silently looking at me; that intriguing smile I had seen before returned.

CHAPTER THIRTEEN: OUT OF THE GLASS

"The cocoon will open, and we will return to the real world," he said. "We will walk out of the glass."

Just as he said the words, the cocoon wall opened, first a crack, not like the opening curtains of light, but a fissure in the wall of light. Behind the light all I could see was blackness. Slowly the light receded and around us, and without seeing him, my other self-stepped behind me and entered me, guiding my every action. Once the wall was gone, the floor disappeared, and I found myself in that same black void I had passed through when I entered the glass. In total silence and with no awareness of direction, I moved my feet. I was walking as if through the dark expanse of space until at last I burst forth into my living room.

I looked at my watch, the second hand began to move. The time on the clock on the wall of my living room had not changed since my leaving. I stood there, relieved to be home, but certain there was more to the journey. A shudder went through me as my other self left me. There we stood, just as we had when this all began.

"What now?" I asked, realizing how tired I found myself and how much I wanted to rest. "I think I had better sit down."

"One more lesson before you do."

"Do I have to do anything? I don't think I have the strength for it. I can't believe how tired I am."

"All you have to do is listen to me." There was a pause as the sun peaked out from behind a lingering cloud and flooded the room with light. "Look around you. Look outside. The sun shines on everything, there are shadows everywhere. Do you see them? People often go through life ignoring their own shadow, afraid of it. See your shadow?" I looked down at the floor where the imprint of my shadow lay, as if resting. "The shadow you cast may seem as fleeting as footprints on the sandy beach, but it is far more important. Your shadow is a constant reminder of the source of light that creates it, and your presence which enables the shadow to appear. If you had never been here, there would never have been a shadow. If you stand in other people's shadow, you never cast a shadow of your own. If you stand in the shade, your shadow is diminished. It is time for you to cast your shadow. It may not make you wealthy, it may not grant you fame, but it will complete you. Like a reflection, your shadow is the reality of your existence. Do you understand?"

"I do." I walked across the room, watching my shadow follow me, moving up and down the contours of the furniture.

"It's time for me to leave this world." His words stunned me.

"What?"

"I'm not leaving you I'm just leaving this world. It's time for me to enter you for the last time. I will now live within you, where I belong, in your sacred center. There you can call upon me for support. Remember, that at your core, you are not at war with those around you, but with yourself. I'll be there to quell the discord and doubt, helping you with your decisions and supporting your actions. You will never be alone again."

"But I thought you were always there?"

"I was, but remember I had to be awakened the same way you had to be awakened. You are very fortunate to have been chosen to have experienced all that you have. You're a good person and now you will be an even better person."

"Can I sit down now I don't feel very good."

"We must complete our task. Come over here and stand behind me." I did as he instructed. "Now, put your arms around my chest and gently hug me."

"I don't want you to go. I need you."

"You will always have me. Every time you see your shadow or look at your reflection in the glass, you will remember me and all that we experienced together."

I walked over to behind him, put my arms out and then linked them together across his chest. I looked down at our shadows on the floor, touching as if we were one.

"Now close your eyes," he said, "and draw my body close to you." I closed my eyes and drew my arms closer together, felt a familiar shudder pass through my body, and realized my arms were now empty. Opening my eyes and looking down, I saw only one shadow, my own; but I knew I was not alone.

EPILOGUE

I'm one who has always preferred to live in the shadows, shying away from the spotlight, stepping onto center stage only when I forced myself. Even then, the credit for the success of those limelight moments has never been mine alone, but one that belongs rightfully to the corporate body of those who labored together. The spotlight has always reminded me that the shadows were the safe place to be. For someone who is awkward in groups, hesitant to mingle with others, an unwilling leader and perennially unsure of himself, the shadows have meant an easy journey through life, one where I did not have to expose my vulnerabilities. Now I write this: *Your shadow is a constant reminder of the source of light that creates it, and your presence which enables the shadow to appear. If you had never been here, there would never have been a shadow. If you stand in other people's shadow, you never cast a shadow of your own. If you stand in the shade, your shadow is diminished. It is time for you to cast your shadow. It may not make you wealthy, it may not grant you fame, but it will complete you.* I suppose in writing this book it is God's way of reminding me to remind myself of who I am and my purpose in life. That understanding has been a long time in coming.

Writing has always been easy for me, a passion, but one I never defined as a passion. It all started in third grade, when every week for months, I wrote a chapter to a fairy tale that my teacher posted on the hallway bulletin board for everyone to read. In high school I wrote a collection of essays (thinking myself a new Emerson, which I am not). In college I wrote and directed my first full-length play. After college as a newspaper reporter I wrote daily to meet deadlines. In seminary I wrote volumes of academic papers every week for three years. For the last forty plus years of ministry I have written a chapter a week to what always seemed an endless book of sermons. In between, there have been more plays, short stories and....

The "and" is hard to explain because I have been in denial about the source and purpose behind the spiritual awakening that produced works that emerged from my pen. Sometime in the 1990s I had the realization that an out-of-body experience from 1967 held far greater significance than I had ever known. Back in those college years I had the honor to participate in an archaeology dig looking for Pre-Colombian artifacts around Upstate New York. For the final two weeks of that summer expedition we were housed in tents on an island in Black Lake in Northern New York. One evening I went off to be by myself and as I lay down on the rocky ledge above the calm waters of Black Lake, I felt myself up in the stars. I could see myself below on the rocky ledge. It was then that a voice spoke to me and said, "You are so small, and you have so much to do." It was over in an instant. The next day I was physically and mentally exhausted. I didn't understand why. When the expedition ended, I realized the only memento I had of the trip was a stone I had dug up in Northern New York.

Four years after the archaeology trip I found myself as a VISTA Volunteer in New Mexico. I really didn't understand why I was there. I spoke no Spanish and had no sense of the history of the Southwest. I was assigned to manage a small community center. To help secure local funds I participated in the United Methodist Church; a safe place since I had grown up Methodist and the church was where many of the local businessmen attended. The memory of the out-of-body experience and the white stone came racing back into my consciousness when in church one Sunday I read on the bulletin cover a quote of Revelation 2: 17: *He who has an ear, let him hear what the Spirit says to the churches. To him who conquers I will give some of the hidden manna, and I will give him a white stone with a new name written on the stone which no one knows except him who receives it.* I had the stone, the message I believed was from God and now all I had to do was determine what it was I was supposed to do.

That brings me back to the 1990s where thoughts began to flow from my pen. Yes, I write everything out long hand. The words came so easily, but I was uncertain what it all meant. In the midst of my struggles to find answers, I had lunch with a former seminary professor, and we discussed a manuscript of mine he had graciously read. He told me he believed I was a modern mystic, someone who could channel God-thoughts that others mind not be able to hear or see. Such a lofty purpose was not one, and still is not one, that I would aspire to; but in reality, one that is gifted by God because God has faith in the recipient's ability to comprehend the message and relate it to others. In the weeks that followed I was forced to ask myself if I had faith in myself and in God to meet the challenge.

The writing continued, then a series of visions and a book discussing them. The preaching continued with a new direction based on my personal perspectives and the messages I was receiving from God. Now has come this new revelation from God, "The Pane of Faith." It's not a vision, but what I would term a "spiritual revelation," God instructing me to write that others might find a new hope and purpose in their lives. The ease with which the words flowed onto the pages are, for me, a testament to venture more often out of the comfortable darkness of the shadows of life and stand in the light and cast my own shadow.

STUDY GUIDE

The suggestion was made that perhaps a study guide might as-sist the reader in a more in-depth examination of the thoughts contained in the book as well as concerning thoughts about their own personal pilgrimage. I am a firm believer that we are all on a pilgrimage or journey throughout our life. That pilgrimage may end in fulfillment or disappointment; but in the final analysis, it is the pilgrimage itself that carries the most significance, for it is in its essence the compilation of all of life's experiences. "The Pane of Faith" is about finding one's way in life, experiencing both the physical and spiritual aspect of life to their conclusion; a conclu-sion of self-realization. For every question here, there may be a dozen more to surface. That's what a pilgrimage is all about: seek-ing answers to questions that arise along the way.

Chapter One: The Beginning

Where are you at this moment on your pilgrimage? When did it begin? Where do you think it is it headed?

Remember, life is filled with multiple pilgrimages that overlap and intersect with each other. One pilgrimage may be no longer that a single day, while the greatest of all pilgrimages encompasses a lifetime.

Are you happy with your life where it is at right now? What would you change?
What do you see in your reflection? Despair? Contentment? What?

Were you to come face-to-face with your inner self, what kind of questions would like answered?

What kind of questions do you have about your past and the decisions you have made?

Chapter Two: Into the Glass

I believe that within every human being there is a spark of God. Embedded deep within us, at our Sacred Center, this spark is our personal connection to God. Individual faith or religious affiliation or lack of faith, is irrelevant, for each human being has this direct connection to God.

What is your perception of what it would be like to be in the presence of God?

How do you see God in your life? What role do you believe God plays in your life?

What kind of experiences have you had that have been benchmarks in your life and how have they changed you?

What people have impacted your life along your pilgrimage pathway?

Chapter Three: Pathway through the Valley

Life is filled with the proverbial hills and valleys. Sometimes we can't seem to see beyond where we are at any given moment. We need to remember that a pilgrimage is about always moving forward, never being static.

When have you felt alone, trapped by circumstances? How did you deal with those feelings?

When has anger taken hold of your actions? How did you ultimately deal with that anger?

What aspects of your personal behavior did you discover in moments of isolation, frustration and anger?

How have you "opened doors of hope" for yourself and others?

Chapter Four: Pathway through the Forest

Joy can be as fleeting as an afternoon shower or as lasting as the infinite grains of sand on the beach. The question for all of us is: Where do we find joy?

Is your life filled with joy? What gives you joy?
What is there in nature that gives you the most joy?
How can you help spread joy to others and how can we "protect" joy and be certain everyone has the opportunity to experience the joy of nature?

Chapter Five: Pathway through the Plain

Often life's journey becomes a flat line. In every direction there seems to be no option other than to continue along an endless plane of existence. As such, life seems to lack variety. That is when you have to look more closely. While the pathway may be narrow, challenging the traveler's every step; even in that you can discover variety.

Major decisions never seem to come easily. How have you felt when faced with major decisions about your life?
When we are conflicted, the process of making decisions is made more difficult. What factors impact your decision-making process?
What does doing "nothing" achieve? What does it say about you if you decide to do nothing?

Chapter Six: Pathway through the Canyon

Faced with seemingly insurmountable obstacles we often retreat to a safe place or the status-quo. However, if we make an effort to seek alternatives, we can find them. If we look back on our life, in retrospect, we can discern the reasons for why we may have been in a specific place at a specific time.

Think about some place you may have been and how that helped define who you have become. Have you ever had to retrace your steps in order to arrive at a point of decision that changed your life?

When have you had to do something out of your comfort zone that at the time you thought impossible but ultimately made a difference in your life?

The notion that we can't know everything is very real. That leaves us with aspects of the unknown and mysteries still to be revealed. What discovery about life would you like to make and how can you go about making it happen?

What mystery in life most interests you and how can you go about learning more about it?

Chapter Seven: Pathway through the Desert

Discerning the difference between dreams and visions can be a daunting task. Although we may not remember them, we all experience dreams, those subconscious thoughts brought to life in our dreams. Visions on the other hand, instead of resurfacing thoughts from our subconscious, are memorable perceptions of things seen that are yet to come. While dreams are generated from within our subconscious, visions are emanated from an outside force, from God.

Have you ever experienced a vision that was the portent of things to come? Remember, visions are often shrouded in imagery that may not be immediately understandable. How have visions impacted your life? Not all of us have the privilege of being recipients of visions, so don't be upset if you have never had what would be described as a vision.

There are times in life when we may feel like we are in the midst of a vast desert or wilderness. Have you ever felt that way? How did you move out of that time and place in your life? What or who helped you along the way? In the desert we can be tricked by a mirage. That forces us to make a decision. How would you decide between two seemingly identical options?

Chapter Eight: Pathway through the Garden

There is the old expression "life is no bed of roses." Life teaches us the reality of that cliché. For some people the "bed of roses" is a thicket of thorns. It's all in how we decide to perceive life. How do you see your life's "garden"?

When has beauty and joy been brought into your life? When has that beauty and joy in your life been taken away?

Have you ever felt "trapped in the gray, colorless world"? How can you work to "re-color" your world?

Chapter Nine: Pathway through the Mountain Cave

Journeys are often taken with another person. The shared experience of a pilgrimage is enhanced by the insight garnered by two or more people who exchange thoughts along the way. However, there are also times when the strength of a single person outweighs that of a group. Sometimes the forward progress of a pilgrimage is quickened when the journey is undertaken alone.

The darkness of a cave is very real and its power over the pilgrim cannot be underestimated. Have you ever been in so dark a place that you lost your way? It may be a physical place or a mental state of mind. How has prayer helped your through those dark times?

When did prayer make a difference for you when it came to making decisions?

Listening to our conscience, that inner voice, is important in everything we do. It helps us choose right over wrong and good over evil. Do you take the time to listen to your inner voice? If not, how can you work to pause more often, so you can better hear your inner voice?

Chapter Ten: Pathway through the Island

Issues of isolation are ever-present in our lives. We may find ourselves walking in circles, never-ending circles of frustration, until we break out of that cycle and find a new course to follow.

While it may seem like solutions appear like a rabbit pulled from a hat, the reality is that solutions do appear for every dilemma. "Every situation has its own oasis."

When have you felt like you were running in circles or on a treadmill going nowhere? How did you resolve that situation? Did finding the "oasis" made you stronger?

Chapter Eleven: Pathway through the Swamp

Swamps can be very threatening environments. The menacing prospect of the hostile surroundings engenders feelings of the sinister and evil. Swamps also provide a rich environment for wildlife, seen and unseen. Here the swamp is the first instance where another lifeform appears yet is never seen. The question may be: is it real or imagined? Is he being pursued by some evil being or by the negative forces of his own imagination?

Have you ever been faced with a life or death decision? How did you feel at the time?

Fear is a powerful, learned emotion, impacting our decision-making process. When have you been truly fearful, if ever? How did you respond? What was the result?

Forces of influence from outside of us challenge us much differently than those of our emotions. How have external forces, such as being threatened by another person or thing, affected you?

How do we learn fear? How do we combat fear in a world of hate, ignorance and distrust? How can we overcome those societal obstacles to make ourselves and our world a better and healthier place in which to live?

Chapter Twelve: Pathway through the Waters

Water is essential to life; it also possesses enormous power. We have to have water not only in our life, but for the growth of all life. We use water for transportation, recreation and agriculture. Along the pilgrimage of life, we can experience periods where we possess no control over our situation. That's the surface response we often employ: things were out of control; I had no control over what was happening. The reality is we do control certain aspects of our life. In every situation we control our free will, thus being able to exercise control over our destiny.

When have you felt you had no control over a situation only to find an answer to resolve what was happening?

How do you balance the potential sacrifice one has to make in saving another against just saving one's self?

How is one reborn spiritually? What needs to happen to your inner being to experience a new life?

What does it mean to be stripped naked of all the trappings of society? To have no mask to hide behind? No clothes? What are we left with when those protective layers are gone?

Chapter Thirteen: Out of the Glass

We go through life as well as a pilgrimage (recognizing that some pilgrimages are of short duration) seeking enlightenment, spiritual awakening or renewal. In the process, along the way, we are changed, strengthened and made more aware of ourselves. Yet, some people refuse to accept change, finding themselves constantly languishing in the dark shadows.

If "your shadow is a constant reminder of the source of the light that creates it," what is that source?

Whose shadows have obscured your shadow? How did you move out of the shadows to create your own shadow, or imprint on the world?

At the end of the pilgrimage we can be made whole. When have you felt the newness, the wholeness, like never before?

In what way can you help explain to others what you have experienced and how you felt at the end of your pilgrimage?